The IEA Health and Welf

Choice in Welfare N

Is There A Third Way?
Essays on the Changing Direction of Socialist Thought

The IEA Health and Welfare Unit

Choice in Welfare No. 46

Is There A Third Way?
Essays on the Changing Direction of Socialist Thought

Michael Novak

Commentaries

Anthony Giddens
John Lloyd
Paul Ormerod

IEA Health and Welfare Unit
London

First published September 1998

The IEA Health and Welfare Unit
2 Lord North St
London SW1P 3LB

© The IEA Health and Welfare Unit 1998

ISBN 0-255 36438-5
ISSN 1362-9565

Typeset by the IEA Health and Welfare Unit
in Bookman 10 point
Printed in Great Britain by
Hartington Fine Arts Ltd, Lancing, West Sussex

Contents

The Authors

Michael Novak is the Director of Social and Political Studies at the American Enterprise Institute in Washington, DC, where he also holds the George Frederick Jewett Chair in Religion and Public Policy. His best known book is *The Spirit of Democratic Capitalism*, 1982, which was widely influential in Poland, Czechoslavakia, and later America during the 1980s. *The New Consensus on Family and Welfare*, 1987, a Seminar Report of which he was the principal author, is considered a watershed study in welfare reform in the US, and in this connection he has been a frequent lecturer at the Institute of Economic Affairs in London. For the originality of his work in theology and economics, he was awarded the Templeton Prize for Progress in Religion at Buckingham Palace in 1994.

Anthony Giddens, the Director of the London School of Economics and Political Science, is the author or editor of more than thirty books in the areas of sociology, politics and social theory, which have been translated into 22 languages. Eight books, including one four-volume study, have been written specifically devoted to Giddens' work. Among his recent books are: *The Consequences of Modernity*, 1989, *Modernity and Self Identity*, 1991, *The Transformation of Intimacy*, 1992, *Beyond Left and Right*, 1994 and *In Defence of Sociology*, 1996. He is also the author of *Sociology*, the world's leading text in the subject. Anthony Giddens was Professor of Sociology and Fellow of King's College Cambridge before coming to the LSE at the beginning of 1997.

John Lloyd is Associate Editor of the *New Statesman* and a writer for the *Financial Times* and *Scotland on Sunday*. His book *Rebirth of a Nation: an Anatomy of Russia* was published in 1998 by Michael Joseph.

Paul Ormerod moved from academic forecasting at the National Institute of Economic and Social Research (NIESR) to the private sector in the early 1980s, setting up the Henley Centre for Forecasting with a group of colleagues. In the early 1990s the Centre was sold to the WPP Group, and since 1995 he has been chairman of Post-Orthodox Economics. His book *The Death of Economics* was published by Faber and Faber in 1994 and has been translated into ten languages. The sequel, *Butterfly Economics*, will be published in November 1998.

Foreword

We can all recall seeing the television pictures of Berliners chipping away at the Berlin Wall with hammers when weeks earlier the border guards would have shot them on sight. For Michael Novak the fall of the Berlin Wall was one of the turning points of the twentieth century. It certainly signalled the collapse of communism, but can we say with equal certainty that it represented the victory of capitalism? Was it a victory for one economic system over another, or the triumph of a wider moral or cultural order? Would it be more accurate to say it was a victory for liberty over totalitarianism, or for democracy over authoritarianism? And where does the collapse of communism leave socialism? It shared many of the same public policy objectives but preferred democracy to authoritarianism.

In Britain there is considerable talk of an emerging 'third way' between capitalism and socialism. Whether the 'third way' will ever amount to anything more than a presentational tactic remains to be seen, but fundamental changes in socialist thought are undoubtedly taking place. Novak's insights into the emerging socialism/social democracy are analysed by three distinguished commentators—Professor Anthony Giddens, John Lloyd and Paul Ormerod—each of whom has already made important contributions to the developing socialist tradition. Michael Novak has the last word in a Rejoinder.

Whether the reader's focus is on 'what kind of capitalism' or 'what kind of socialism' there is much to be learnt from the authors' exchange.

David G. Green

Author's Note

This paper was originally prepared for a conference on welfare reform in Italy, sponsored by the publishing house Mondadori in the spring of 1997. My assignment was to present a provocative point of view, outside the European social democratic framework, in order to encourage looser and more imaginative ways of approaching admitted social needs. It was understood by the sponsors that my own point of view is not (in American parlance) 'libertarian' nor precisely what is called in Britain 'New Right'. More than most American libertarians, I argue in principle for political and moral constraints upon economic activities, and for carefully designed and well-checked interventions on the part of the state. I argue in particular for a modified version—highly modified these days—of the welfare state. I call this approach 'democratic capitalism' (rather than democratic socialism or social democracy), because I see a dynamic, creative, inventive economy as the main hope of improvement in the lot of the poor. In America, this point of view is widely called 'neo-conservative', a term that connotes conversion from an earlier period as a social democrat.

Perhaps the best statement of my views on welfare, and of the empirical materials on which they are based, is found in The New Consensus on Family and Welfare, *a report of a seminar of experts of right and left, of which I was the principal drafter, published jointly by Marquette University and the American Enterprise Institute in 1987. This report, warmly received both in the US Senate (Democratic) and in the White House (Republican) at that time, is sometimes discussed as the watershed document in the new thinking that led to the Welfare Reform Act of 1996 signed by President Clinton. Among the twenty signatories of the report were such well-known liberals as Alice M. Rivlin, Franklin D. Raines, and Robert D. Reischauer, as well as conservatives such as Lawrence Mead, Richard P. Nathan, and Charles Murray.*

A more philosophical/theological exposition of 'democratic capitalism' (but with very little to say about welfare as such) may be found in The Spirit of Democratic Capitalism (1982), *published in Britain in its second, revised edition in 1991.*

Michael Novak
March 1998

The Crisis of Social Democracy

Michael Novak

In the end each nation is no more than a flock of timid and hardworking animals with government as its shepherd.

Alexis de Tocqueville[1]

FOR Alan Greenspan, Chairman of the Federal Reserve Board in the United States, the decisive economic event of our time was the collapse of the Berlin Wall in late 1989. The outside light which then flooded East Germany revealed the outcome of the forty-year experiment in socialist economics, in stark contrast to the capitalist economics in West Germany. Both parts of Germany had shared the same culture and history; both had been reduced to ruins by World War II; both had had to start over from ground zero. 'It is as near as social scientists ever get to observing a controlled experiment', Greenspan says. For the hypothesis that socialist economic theory is superior to Western theories of political economy, the results were devastating.

Ten years after the fall of the Wall, even though heavily subsidised, East Germany is still a very poor cousin of West Germany. The most dramatic costs of the socialist experiment are measured in the loss of human capital, including the work ethic, entrepreneurship, and habits of risk, trust, and creativity.

Moreover, the collapse of 'real existing socialism' in its stronghold in the former Soviet Union has had a ripple effect through the structures of international socialism elsewhere. For it demonstrated to all that as an *economic* theory socialism is seriously flawed, and that the socialist analysis of capitalist economies was also incorrect.

This collapse of the *economic* principles of socialism affected not only Communism but all those other doctrines and ideals that rest in part on socialist economic theories, including social democracy. Communist and socialist parties around the world hurried to change their official names, usually to some euphemism such as 'social democratic'. Yet even in those nations

1

having a genuine claim to the good name of social democracy, birth rates are falling; senior citizens are living longer; advances in health care grow ever more costly; and the ratio of active workers to pensioners has already dropped to nearly three to one or worse, and is projected to continue dropping rapidly.[2] In these circumstances social democratic parties are adopting economic policies favouring enterprise, job-creation, profits, reinvestment and personal incentives.

The New Terrain

Thus, the election of Tony Blair in Britain in 1997, and the conception of New Labour which enabled him to triumph, far from vindicating social democracy, in fact confirmed its transformation, and in a way that has important consequences for Britain and, indeed, all of Europe. Many commentators in Europe and elsewhere have noted that the triumph of Tony Blair may in one sense be regarded as the triumph of Margaret Thatcher. Blair's New Labour has adopted a political project (and a social ideal) inconceivable for Labour fifteen, ten, or even five years ago. After her election in 1979, Margaret Thatcher demonstrated that the world had changed fundamentally and radically. By launching Great Britain on a trajectory of growth and opportunity that lasted, with some inevitable setbacks, for twenty years, the Iron Lady weaned New Labour from a sterile and punitive redistributionism, on the one hand, and from the enervating Nanny State, on the other. She taught Blair the importance of growth, opportunity, and incentives. Only so could Tony Blair ride to triumph.

It appears that many (although not all) on the European left have learned this lesson, including the recently elected Socialist Party in France. Leaders of the European left are accustomed to lead social change, not to follow, and in the main to change their own course rather than to fail. As long as they can protect (as they see it) the *ends* they have in view—equality, compassion, amelioration of the lot of the poor, etc.—they fairly easily adjust to new *means*: new tactics, new strategies, even new visions of the future.

Consider the words of John Gray of Oxford University, one of the most perceptive political thinkers in Europe, writing in *The Times Literary Supplement*:

Europe's social democratic regimes were established during an era of closed economies. They rested on the capacity of sovereign states to limit the free movement of capital and production through exchange controls and tariffs. They cannot survive in an environment in which capital and production exercise unfettered global mobility.[3]

Tony Blair, Gray argues, is important because several years ago he grasped how deeply Europe's social democracies are mired in policies that belong to an irrecoverable past. The muck and mire in which social democracy is stuck, according to Gray, consists of three parts. First, once technological innovation begins wiping out entire occupations (and even industries), a labour market anchored in institutions of job security is not sustainable. Second, pension schemes that tie benefits to a single employer offer flimsy security in this new era, in which no one can be sure of having the same job across a working lifetime. Third, welfare institutions that are designed primarily to compensate people for failure and punish them for success 'are supremely unfitted for an age of globalisation'. From these points Gray concludes: 'Unless Europe's social democracies reform themselves deeply and swiftly, they will be blown away by the gale of global competition'.

If John Gray is correct, the premises of the social compact that followed after World War II have been thrown into doubt. No wonder there is much social pessimism on the continent. No wonder the prospect of 'globalisation' agitates many intelligent Europeans. Their deepest worry is not just high unemployment. Nor is it the towers of debt mounting on all sides. It is a growing doubt about the basic postwar settlement.

After generations of denigrating capitalism, especially American capitalism, many of Europe's intellectuals are for the first time doubting their traditional understanding of the word 'social' —socialism, social democracy, social justice, social compact. Suddenly, they do not like one form of socialisation; they do not like 'globalisation'.

In the United States, by contrast, one most often hears optimism about globalisation. (To be sure, we have our own doomsayers, economic nationalists wedded to the memories of an isolationist Fortress America. Noisy though they be, however, they do not command either political party.) The rising stock market reveals the current American temper well enough, but an anecdote may sharpen the picture. When, in May 1997, the Dow

Jones Industrial average stood at an all-time high of 6,500 and the papers were predicting an imminent serious 'correction', two economic journalists made a bet in the presence of a dozen others, that by the last day of the year 2000 the market would stand at 11,000; and no one at the dinner thought the bet unreasonable. The basis for their bet: globalisation.

Several months later, the Asian crisis became evident and predictions of an impending correction in the stock market poured out unabated. Meanwhile, most Americans continued to talk and dream of unparalleled opportunity. Such talk may well be wildly mistaken. Anecdotes prove nothing. They do illustrate, however, a recurrent experience: regarding globalisation, the difference in psychological climate between the United States and Europe is palpable. (Britain, with its far-flung Commonwealth connections, may share something of the US optimism, while still being close enough to continental Europe to share the sense of strain.)

As long ago as 1835, Alexis de Tocqueville pointed out that, compared to Europeans, Americans delight in risks, opportunities, adventures, dreams. Even today Americans delight in the striking economic success (despite the recent 'Asian crisis') of capitalist models among what Gray called 'the highly literate and numerate societies of East Asia', and look now for new opportunities as the lessons behind that crisis are learned. They also delight in 'the enormous expansion of world markets consequent on the Soviet collapse and economic reform in China', and in the remarkable advances in leading sectors of Latin America (such as Chile). Some Americans conclude that, for the first time in history, the vast natural resources of the entire planet—in remote Russia, in China—will come on stream for the benefit of the common good of all humanity.

How can one explain this optimism to Europeans? In 1979, recall, President Carter and many others saw only malaise, 'stagflation' and decline. Since Ronald Reagan launched foundational economic reforms in 1981, however, the US economy has grown by more than one-third—added the equivalent of the whole economy of Germany, East and West, to its base—and given birth to new technologies and whole new industries never seen before. The computer industry, in 1981 insignificant, is now the nation's largest. The ranks of America's employees have swollen by more than 30 million; the unemployment rate is the lowest in 30 years.

This optimism about economic prospects is not partisan; Clinton and Gore have made it their own.

The Cultural Crisis

Given our economic dynamism, we in the United States are nonetheless preoccupied with a different sort of crisis: a cultural crisis. Whereas in Europe the *social contract* of the era since World War II is in need of urgent reform, in the United States most analysts argue that we need urgent *cultural* reform. We need cultural reform not only in the realm of movies and television and popular music, but also in the arena of public and private moral life. Indeed, most Americans concur that the free society, to maintain its vitality, depends upon a healthy *moral ecology* (if one may so speak). *A free society is primarily a moral achievement.* Free institutions cannot be maintained, certainly their vigour cannot be maintained, on just any moral basis whatsoever. How can a people incapable of self-government in personal life, James Madison once asked, prove capable of self-government in public life?

From both sides of the Atlantic, therefore, although from different patterns of evidence, our common civilisation is becoming aware of mortal dangers. The structural constitution of the modern state faces two witheringly severe tests over time, and if it fails to meet either of those tests, the state may all too easily shatter on the rocks. The first test is the test of outer reality—economics, what is happening in other states, technological developments, globalisation, etc. The second test is the test of inner reality—what is happening to the morality and the morale of citizens. Europe most fears the first; America the second.

A few words about the second test, the inner test, may be useful because less familiar in public discourse. Two decades ago, on a given Monday the Shah of Iran presided over the fifth largest army in the world, and by the subsequent Friday, after a sudden Islamic uprising, his army laid down its arms and he was deposed: a lesson in the power of the human spirit over arms. One decade ago, the events of June 1989 in Beijing and then of November 1989 in Hungary, Czechoslovakia, East Germany, Rumania and elsewhere, again demonstrated the great power of spiritual factors. Solzhenitsyn had written 18 years earlier that one word of truth is more powerful than many armed divisions; this prediction unfolded inexorably before our eyes.

Another aspect of the cultural crisis might best be revealed in a parable. In California, in the late 1960s, Gunnar Myrdal assured a public seminar that social democracy (the apple of his eye) would never weaken the virtues of the Swedish people. Years later, he issued a sorrowful public statement that, regrettably, the morals of Sweden had been weakened, perhaps irreparably; many were calling in sick when they were not sick, or declaring disability for 'bad backs', etc. Similarly in the US: 'the state is pushing all that money out there', runs the new rationalisation. 'It would be naive of me not to claim my share'. Dependency on state subsidies has grown in the last thirty years. That is not, of course, the only source of moral corruption in our time (along with being the source of much good); the cultural sources of corruption are many.

That the morals of the people of the United States have been corrupted for the worse during our lifetime is abundantly evident in innumerable statistical profiles: violent crime up 600 per cent since 1965; births out of wedlock up 600 per cent, etc. Robert Bork presents some of these indicators in *Slouching Toward Gomorrah*.[4] The Secretary of Health of the United States estimated in 1990 that 40 to 70 per cent of all premature deaths in the US are *behavioural*—that is, due to avoidable, self-damaging personal behaviours (excessive drinking, drugs, disordered sex, smoking, failing to exercise, poor diet, habits of violent behaviour, etc.) Independent of a moral analysis (even if from plural points of view), the public policy costs of these unprecedented trends are stubborn and immense. The costs of crime prevention, health, and welfare have rocketed upwards. Deficits burdening future generations are incurred. Worse, current taxpayers are coerced into subsidising self-destructive behaviours on the part of others.

Although consensus is widespread among policy experts both in Europe and in the United States about the *financial* crisis of the welfare state—its fiscal unsustainability and the impending implosion of accumulated debt that will greet a new generation in the not-too-distant future—it is the *spiritual* crisis of the welfare state that is the more severe. For the most important form of capital is human capital: the active, intelligent, creative citizen. If we are destroying our human capital, our civilisation is in mortal danger.

Even years ago, Alexis de Tocqueville gave early warning about the triumph of the ideal of equality over liberty: 'I am trying to imagine under what novel features despotism may appear in the world', he wrote in 1835. He imagined a type of 'orderly, gentle, peaceful slavery', which under the name of equality had come to be accepted as endurable. Moved by compassion for its subjects, government:

> provides for their security, foresees and supplies their necessities, facilitates their pleasures, manages their principal concerns, directs their industry, makes rules for their testaments, and divides their inheritances. It covers the whole of social life with a network of petty, complicated rules that are both minute and uniform, through which even men of the greatest originality and the most vigorous temperament cannot force their heads above the crowd. It does not break men's will, but softens, bends, and guides it; it seldom enjoins, but often inhibits, action; it does not destroy anything, but prevents much being born; it is not at all tyrannical, but it hinders, restrains, enervates, stifles, and stultifies so much that in the end each nation is no more than a flock of timid and hardworking animals with the government as its shepherd.[5]

This is the nightmare that haunts Americans.

Accusations Against the Welfare State

It is obvious to us in the United States—certainly, to those of us born into poor families, in the midst of the Depression of the 1930s—that the welfare state has done much good; indeed, has been in many ways indispensable. From programmes of rural electrification to building new college campuses (on the average of one every two weeks from 1948 until 1978); from programmes of farm credit to mortgage assistance; from food stamps to employment and work training programmes; from income supplements (social security) to Medicare for senior citizens—in countless ways, federal and state governments have helped virtually all citizens to find better lives.

The argument today is not, then, *whether* to have welfare programmes but *of what kind*, in order to meet new conditions and to correct deficiencies and unintended consequences that sixty years of experience (since Franklin Delano Roosevelt's 'New Deal') have brought to light. In addition, a sharp distinction is often made between the philosophy underlying the New Deal and the quite different philosophy underlying the 'Great Society'

launched by President Lyndon B. Johnson in 1964. The New Deal
was based—to state the issue much too roughly—on traditional
American values; the Great Society, it is alleged, introduced a
new morality. Under the former, for instance, some 98 per cent
or so of recipients of Aid to Families with Dependent Children
(AFDC) were widows; under the latter, nearly all benefits now go
to divorced, separated, and (no questions asked, no demands
made) never-married women. The spirit of the Great Society programmes is both to be 'non-judgmental' and to hand out benefits
without concern for reciprocity from the recipient, as if in plain
and simple 'entitlement'.

Because of such practices, accusations such as the following
have become more frequent. First, the benefits of the welfare
state are too easy to obtain and too attractive to resist. We come
to feel (by a multitude of rationalisations) that the state 'owes' us
benefits, to which we are as 'entitled' as anybody else. Whether
we need it or not, we would be foolish not to take what is so
abundantly offered. In this way, the welfare state corrupts
us—and loses control over its own mounting expenditures.

Second, in an exaggerated reaction against 'individualism', US
liberals (in Europe, social democrats) not only tend to overem-
phasise 'community', but also too uncritically to identify 'community' with the 'public sector' (the state). To act as the primary
agent of community, they typically prefer the official programmes
of the administrative state to existing voluntary programmes.
Some do this even while warning themselves against the dangers
embedded in bureaucratic methods (that these deny the subjec-
tivity of the person, for example). They say that a national project
generates a greater sense of 'belonging' to a caring national
community.

Two results seem to follow. First, the subjective sense of
personal responsibility slowly atrophies, eventually breeding the
'sluggishness' in welfare states on which, for instance, the
Second Vatican Council commented in 1965, even while praising
the welfare state.[6] Next, the administrative state steadily swal-
lows up most of the functions that used to be exercised by civil
society.[7] Mediating institutions become enfeebled.[8] Thus, the
principle of subsidiarity is continually violated, as the higher
levels crush the lower.

One of the most respected social commentators in the United
States, Irving Kristol, cites Hegel on the descent from the virility

of Republican Rome to the decadence of Imperial Rome: 'the image of the state as a product of his activity disappeared from the soul of the citizen'. It is far worse today, Kristol holds:

> Today, it is the mission of the welfare state to convince the citizen that he is the product of the state's activity, that he is an importuning subject of the state, no longer a citizen in the classical sense. The fully developed welfare state is a modern version of the feudal castle, guarded by moats and barriers, and offering security and shelter to the loyal population that gathers round it.[9]

The peoples of the welfare state have traded the inheritance of liberty that had been won for them at enormous cost in exchange for a promise of security—a promise that can no longer be met.

The welfare state softens the morals of some of its recipients, one accusation goes; another says that it penalises the creativity and hard work of those who pay for it, too; a third, that it discourages employers from creating new jobs.

Statistics do not directly reveal how subtly this last process works. Permit me again to tell a story. In 1997, an Italian professor was talking with his barber, asking him why, since he was so busy, the barber didn't hire more help. The barber stopped cutting his hair and became agitated. 'I would like to hire somebody!' he insisted. 'But I have taken my pencil and counted up the costs. By the time I pay wages, and every kind of benefit, and every kind of tax, I end up *losing* money, and that doesn't count headaches and aggravation or my time! I would like to hire someone, I am getting old, but I can't! *Che stupidaggine!*'

Among the new critics of the welfare state is a surprising one, the Pope (surprising because in Europe Catholic social thought is widely believed to be closer to social democratic thought than to laissez-faire). The opinions of a Pope may cut little ice in Britain, but since Catholics in several European nations tend to lean in a social democratic direction, papal criticisms of the welfare state, such as the following, shed an interesting light on the coming crisis:

> By intervening directly and depriving society of its responsibility, the Social Assistance State leads to (1) a loss of human energies and (2) an inordinate increase of public agencies, which (3) are dominated more by bureaucratic ways of thinking than by concern for serving clients, and (4) are accompanied by an enormous increase in spending [enumeration added].[10]

In displacing the action of human charity, in other words, the Social Assistance State displaces the 'little platoons' that give life its properly human scale, and generates a 'mass society', impersonal, ineffectual, counter-productive, and suffocating of the human spirit. In displacing the vitalities of a thick and self-governing civil society, the Social Assistance State diminishes the realm of responsible personal action.

Without question, the modern welfare state has done much good, particularly for the elderly, and yet in many nations its results for younger adults, and especially for marriage and family life, have been highly destructive. The proportion of children born out of wedlock has hit unprecedented levels in many nations, including the United States, Great Britain, and Sweden.[11] Many take this to be the most devastating piece of evidence in the case against the welfare state. Quite unintentionally, *contrary* to its intention, social democracy seems to injure families even in cultures in which the family has been the primary basis of strength. 'Fifty years ago', adds Irving Kristol, 'no advocate of the welfare state could imagine it might be destructive of that most fundamental social institution, the family. But it has been, with a poisonous flowering of those very social pathologies—crime, illegitimacy, drugs, divorce, sexual promiscuity—that it was assumed the welfare state would curb if not eliminate'.

The Family and Welfare

It was precisely to examine such accusations that the aforementioned Seminar on Family and Welfare, carefully chosen to represent both the right and the left, met together for more than one year. After considerable effort, we reached consensus on what had been achieved by welfare programmes during the preceding twenty years, between 1965 and 1985—what had gone right, and what had gone wrong. We also reached agreement on a long list of recommendations for reform. We hoped that we might turn the thinking of both major political parties in a new direction.

No one could deny that the lot of the elderly (those over 65) had improved enormously since 1965. By 1985 a huge majority of those over 65 lived in their own homes (a sign of their health and independent spirits) and most of their homes were mortgage-free. The percentage living in poverty had been reduced to single digits, and this residuum was due mainly to failures to connect to existing programmes, of which they were not taking advantage. The elderly were certainly living longer; by 1985, in fact, there were millions more of them than in earlier generations. Indeed, a *new* concern suddenly emerged for what were now called the 'elderly elderly', the suddenly enlarged cohort of those over 85.[12]

The picture is quite different for young adults between 18 and 64, whose situation was far worse in 1985 than in 1965. Violent crime was 600 per cent higher; family structure was far more deeply wounded; the morale of many was far less hopeful. Moreover, our seminar discovered that the worst sufferings usually ascribed to 'poverty' were, in fact, associated with family break-up. This discovery arose accidentally. In correlating various statistical tables, our research noted that: (a) of all married-couple families in the US, only 6.7 per cent were poor. In other words, the simple fact of being married gave Americans a 93 per cent chance of not being poor. These chances were further improved by two more factors: (b) completion of secondary school (which is both wholly subsidised and mandatory) and (c) full-time employment at any job, even a minimum-wage job.[13]

This glimpse of the stunning effectiveness of such fundamentals as marriage, education, and employment in reducing poverty was next matched by a closer inspection of the disabilities involved, in the United States, at least, in the lot of being a single mother. Such single moms and their children were the largest group of the US poor and the fastest-growing group. In addition, their children were at far greater risk of not finishing school; not being employed or even employable; having a greater number of health problems; and being involved in the criminal justice system. The picture was far better, of course, for divorced and separated mothers, who tended to be rather more mature at the time of the divorce and separation. Such older single women tended in far higher proportions to find jobs and go off welfare within two years of going on it, and to be quite successful with their children. For the younger women, especially those who were never married, all the statistical profiles offered a bleaker prospect.

Indeed, our research turned up a group of about four million Americans between the ages of eighteen and thirty whose most serious problem was 'dependency' rather than 'poverty'. We gave the term 'dependency' a fairly precise meaning: young and healthy adults who are dependent upon the public purse; and, second, unable to fulfill their obligation toward others in their family, younger and older, who would normally be dependent upon them.[14] In other words, they were not acting, perhaps through no fault of their own, as independent, self-sustaining citizens, on whom their own children could depend.

In addition to this, studies revealed a pronounced tendency for such persons to be caught in a *cycle of dependency*; that is, although they might be off welfare for a year or two, they tended to have frequent bouts of dependency on the public purse and their children also tended to be dependent upon the public purse. This pattern flew against the American expectation of upward mobility. It showed that a substantial number of persons—about four million, plus their children—were not seizing the opportunity to rise out of poverty; on the contrary, they seemed to be stuck in it. This indicated something seriously wrong in the social order.   Meanwhile, millions of new immigrants who arrived on American shores poorer than the American poor, often without the knowledge of English, tended to seize opportunities and move out of poverty within four or five years. By contrast, the healthy young Americans trapped in dependency had considerably more spending money (from the public purse) and considerably less prospect of moving out of dependency. They seemed to be caught in what Hilaire Belloc and Friedrich Hayek, from quite different points of view, had described as a kind of 'serfdom'.

The legions of the dependent were especially concentrated in the poverty districts of the nation's 100 largest cities. They seemed impervious to the efforts of the War on Poverty to improve their conditions; indeed, their appearance in social history seemed to *coincide* with the War on Poverty. To be perfectly clear about this, we found little evidence that the War on Poverty *caused* the new dependency among so many. But there was a great deal of evidence for the judgment that the War on Poverty was not making much headway in reducing their numbers. Their lot seemed to be getting worse. They were 'losing ground'.

Perhaps the most interesting part of our study consisted of the seventy or so positive recommendations for action on which we agreed.[15] Many of these are now the subjects of social experiments in the fifty states, and some by the federal government. Indeed, the national Welfare Reform Act of 1996 went into effect in the autumn of 1997. Since its passage, welfare roles have shrunken voluntarily (before sanctions were phased in) by significant percentages in every state—as much as 30-40 per cent. This means far more welfare funding is now available for further experiments and new initiatives. Although much heartened by initial indications, we are, of course, waiting to see the full results, well aware that even the best intended reforms have unintended consequences.

From State to Civil Society

The great guiding theme of the twentieth century was provided by Hegel: the state as the embodiment of human desire and human action; the state imagined as beneficent, compassionate, and noble.

Yet the state, obviously, is neither the only nor the best instrument of the common good. Not only the totalitarian state, but also the welfare state, falls far short of the dreams that millions vested in the state during this century. To their credit, the welfare states of the Atlantic community have greatly eased the burdens of the impoverished peoples who emerged from the Depression of the 1930s and the ruins of World War II, and introduced them to unprecedented levels of prosperity, a significant gain in quality of life and increase in longevity for the elderly, and a broad array of liberties and rights. Nonetheless, its moral and financial costs, there is wide recognition, are unsustainable. Its aims and methods must be radically renegotiated.

Although Tony Blair has recognised the problem, it is not clear as yet what he will imagine as the way out, or what goal he will present as the new and better conception. It is not clear that other European social democrats yet recognise the problem.

In such an axial period as ours, it is of great practical importance to go back to first principles. A return to first principles is a kind of revolution—re + volvere—and in this case it seems to be the only kind that has a hope of working. This involves a review of many seeming simplicities.

For instance, the first fundamental question is this: what *is* a free society worthy of free men and women? Can it be agreed that a free society is first of all a project in self-government, in which self-starting and provident citizens, in order to secure their own rights to liberty and to promote the common good, come together to form a government through their own consent? Since the main idea of an experiment in self-government is that people ought to be free to do for themselves all that they can do for themselves, in their own associations and communities, independently of the state, they must keep the government strictly limited. 'Conservatives' will tend to stress the limits; social democrats will favour generous interpretations of the necessities. Both tendencies, each checked by the other, contribute to the common good.

This is no place for a further discourse on government, but at least a few sentences are necessary if we are to develop a common view about the character of the free citizen. A *citizen* is quite different from a *subject* (as in 'subject of the Austro-Hungarian Empire', like my grandparents). The citizen belongs to the class of sovereigns, the possessors of ultimate power. In the free society, the principal repository of power is the personal responsibility of citizens. If things are not going well, it is up to the citizen to organise an association or a movement that tries to get them back on the right track.

The virtue of *social justice*, in this context, is the habit of forming associations to improve the good of the city. The virtue of social justice, then, is 'social' in two senses. Its aim is the improvement in some respect of the city—the whole nation or a locality within it. Second, its practice entails learning skills such as association, co-operation, and how to inspire and organise others; clearly, *social* skills.

As Tocqueville pointed out, the habit of forming associations is the first law of democracy.[16] No free associations, no genuine democracy. Forming associations is the first task of social justice. Self-government is exercised through the associations formed by free persons. The exercise of this habit is one of the primary political responsibilities of the citizen. It is wrong to identify social justice solely or even principally with the state, as some activists seem to do; social justice is the virtue that energizes the free associations of civil society. Of course, some citizens will use their associations to lobby for government programmes or reforms. The principle of social justice is ideologically neutral, and is practised on both left and right.

The citizen also has serious economic responsibilities. Since human capital is the primary form of capital, the human person is the chief economic resource of every nation. In the economy of free societies, the acting person is the principal dynamo. From the imagination, creativity and initiative of acting persons, economic associations are put together and corporations are formed. The inventiveness and enterprise of acting persons generate both new goods and services, and new ways to deliver them.

The political economy of the free society, therefore, depends to an unprecedented degree on the personal responsibility and associational skills (political and economic) of its citizens. This is the heart of any experiment in self-government.

Public policies that obstruct, weaken, or remove personal responsibility are oppressive to citizens; they are also destructive of the experiment in self-government. Unintended as it may be, it is impossible to doubt that the welfare state has begun to have this effect. Further, isn't it the case that social democrats for some years concentrated more energy on helping the needy than on generating growth and opportunity? Valued equality higher than liberty? Gave higher priority to redistribution than to incentives that reward achievement? In recent years, fortunately, it appears that the social democratic ideal is being adjusted to take greater account of personal initiative and personal responsibility.

Thus, social democrats now have a chance to take a large step forward, and make the project of self-government their own. If this is what Tony Blair intends, his progress will be well worth studying. Whether or not he intends it—or achieves it—this is a project that, for the sake of the future of the free society in Europe, *someone* must undertake to lead.

The main outline of this project is simple enough to state: what the free world needs, rapidly, is a devolution of significant responsibilities from centralised bureaucracies to citizens, alone and in their multiple associations. *Devolution* is the key word: Devolution from the state to civil society. Devolution, also, from central governments to the regions and localities. Devolution to centres of responsibility closer to the immediate practical knowledge that separates realism from irrational bureaucratic edict. The main theme is devolution from state to civil society —from bureaucrats to citizens and their civic associations in every sphere, including the family and religious associations, economic associations and political associations, and artistic and scientific associations and other social groups of various types and purposes. (I am not denying that there is a simultaneous reorganisation of larger international structures, both regional and global, only insisting that these not become oblivious to energies from below.)

Obviously, the state cannot and should not simply 'wither away'. Obviously, too, some elements of the welfare state will continue to be necessary, especially in continental-sized, highly mobile, flexible economies. Nonetheless, it was always a mistake to think that the chief or even sole way of fulfilling the social nature of man is through the state and its collectivist activities.[17] The state comprises only one small slice of an authentic human social life, an important one, but far from being either the heart or the whole of the matter. Moreover, it is wrong to allow the state to seize primacy over civil society. The state is not the master but the servant. The welfare state must be kept in due perspective and tight limits.

Through which public policies can this devolution be carried out over the next generation? With all these points—some, perhaps, painfully obvious—social democrats may well be in rough agreement. Can they walk a few more steps? First some general principles; then three practical policies.

Seven Principles of Devolution

It is wise and useful to refocus the goals we are trying to reach.

First, the overarching aim is to carry through the historic project of self-government. To achieve this aim, we need to raise up large numbers of strong, independent, creative, civic-minded and above all responsible citizens, without whom this project is dead. A negative way of stating this aim is that we must reduce the dependency, passivity, and irresponsibility now widespread in our societies.

Second, it is most efficient to nourish strong families, for the family is the formative institution of strong personalities. Nearly all individuals can be reached through public policies that strengthen the independence of families and heighten their incentives for responsible behaviour.

Third, it is crucial to nourish in all spheres of life—and not to oppress (as most governments do)—personal habits of initiative, creativity, and enterprise. This is the path of human vitality. It is also the path that most closely conforms human beings to the image of their Creator.

Fourth, a necessary instrument of creativity is a capital fund, and so it ought to be the goal of public policy to help every family accumulate a capital fund to transfer across the generations. For more than a hundred years, social reformers have concentrated attention on *income maintenance*. Henceforward, that may be not nearly so creative a focus as emphasis on family *capital formation*.

Fifth, the path of family capital formation is a useful route out of poverty and other vulnerabilities for individuals; but it also relieves the state treasury of insupportable burdens.

Sixth, after decades of centralisation, it is necessary to devolve as many decisions as practical from national bureaucracies to individuals, or at least to local centres. A more creative balance between national and local must be restored. (This 'balance' implies that, in some matters, intervention from above is highly useful for the common good.)

And, seventh, it is necessary to simplify government rules and regulations, especially regarding taxation and the conduct of economic activities. Every complexity in the tax and regulatory code is both a veil blocking transparency and an occasion of corruption. What you want more of (growth, for example), do not heavily tax.

Once these seven principles are firm and clear in the mind, many citizens will have many practical ideas about how to proceed. Here are three recommendations of my own. I state them in general terms, without the specifics by which to adapt them to different national situations and practical circumstances.

Three Policy Proposals

1. Pension Reform: Chile has shown that the traditional method of paying the pensions of elderly citizens can be altered peacefully and quickly, in fulfilment of all the general principles mentioned above. An entire bureaucracy was made to disappear; government involvement in pensions was simplified; individual persons and families accrued an unprecedented degree of independence and wealth; and Chile's national savings rate has become one of the highest in the world.

What I like best about Chile's new system is that the funds in a family head's pension fund that he may not exhaust in his lifetime are inherited by his family. Thus, pensions become a capital asset for the entire family, not solely an income maintenance scheme valid only for as long as the pensioner lives. This heightens the incentive to invest more of your lifetime earnings in your pension fund, for your family's sake.

Essentially, Chilean pension law is now simple: every wage-earner is obliged to invest a stated fraction of his income in a tax-exempt pension plan in one of a government-approved list of mutual investment funds. That fund is vested in his person and follows him from job to job, wherever he goes. Both freedom and creativity are enhanced; personal incentives are improved; families are strengthened; and the prosperity of the whole nation benefits by a huge jump in the national savings rate.

Senator Daniel Patrick Moynihan, a Democrat, has recently proposed a highly limited but important step in this direction; he has had a long career as reformer of the US public pension system.[18]

2. *Medical Savings Accounts*: Here, too, in an effort to fulfill the seven general principles listed above, every citizen ought to be required by law to establish a medical savings fund, in which an obligatory proportion of his earnings would by law be invested in a private account. This account would be tax-exempt, personally vested and portable—it would belong to the citizen and his (or her) family. A portion of the fund would be deducted each month to purchase 'catastrophic insurance', at a relatively 'high deductible' (say, in the US, about $1,500).[19] The remainder would be withdrawn as needed for routine medical expenses. Whatever the individual or family does not spend during their lives remains as an inheritance, a capital fund, for the next generation.

What I like best about this policy is that it greatly reduces the government health bureaucracy, replaces it with personal responsibility, and dramatically alters the incentives of citizens and the location of decision-making power in the health profession. Most of the burden of medical costs on national budgets is removed. Responsibility is restored to individual citizens. Instead of a zero-sum game, medical insurance becomes another way of accumulating a family inheritance. If, God forbid, the family's medical accounts are exhausted by accidents or illnesses, their catastrophic insurance covers their needs.

3. *A Simplified Proportional Income Tax*: Just as Chile has demonstrated that the old-age pension bureaucracy can be disbanded, to the benefit of the common good; and just as medical savings accounts offer a way of dramatically reducing if not eliminating the health care bureaucracy; so also it is possible to simplify national income taxes so as to virtually eliminate

another bureaucracy—and certainly to eliminate its arbitrariness, arrogance, obscurantism, favouritism and corruption. The instrument for doing so is to simplify the tax code in a radical way.

It is well known that tax *revenues*, the actual money governments take in, are by no means identical to tax *rates*, the percentage to be contributed to government. If rates are very high, citizens alter their behaviour so as to pay less than predicted. There are many strategies for doing this, some legitimate, others illegal and/or immoral. A government can set rates *lower* and, nonetheless, bring in revenues that are *higher*. And, of course, rates set too high have been known to reduce revenues substantially.

Therefore, let the government establish one fixed rate for all income from whatever source—at, say, 20 per cent.[20] Next, exempt from income taxes all families in the bottom half of the income distribution, by the following method. To each parent in the family, allow a substantial exemption, and to each child (dependent) allow one-half of that exemption.

In the United States, for example, an exemption of $12,000 for each parent and $6,000 for each of two children would exempt from income the first $36,000 earned by families of four. Since the median income of all US families is approximately $36,000, that means that half of all families would be exempt from income taxes. That in itself would be an enormous simplification.

In this respect, such a reform is family-friendly. It would apply to all families, and protect family income for the cost of child-rearing. Grandparents who live in the household as dependents would also bring with them another exemption. This would make them a financial asset or at least much lighten the burden of caring for them, while enabling families to benefit by their presence.

I also like the fact that, while exempting the poor, the tax is strictly proportional to income. The poor and most of the working class are exempted from income taxes altogether. As for the middle class and the rich, the more they earn, the more taxes they pay. The rate remains the same, but the actual tax payment on an additional $10,000 of income ($2,000) is far lower than the actual tax payment on an additional $100,000 of income ($20,000). Holding the same rates for all is highly likely to increase compliance and transparency, and to reduce evasion and corruption.

The flat tax—I prefer to call it the proportional tax, to empha-sise that everyone pays taxes in proportion to their income and according to the *same* proportion (the quintessence of fair-ness)—is, of course controversial. The American Enterprise Institute has mounted a long series of debates on the flat tax and its chief rivals (the national sales tax; Minority Leader Gephardt's reformed set of five 'progressive' levels; and others).[21]

One of the main objections to the proportional or flat tax, suggested above, is that it is not 'progressive'. This is the main objection Minority Leader Gephardt articulates on behalf of his five-rate alternative. Why does he insist on progressive rates? 'No arguments', he says, 'just a gut feeling' that the rich and the poor should pay at different rates; somehow that seems more fair.[22] He boasts that, in his plan, 70 per cent of all taxpayers would pay a maximum rate of only 10 per cent.

Table 1
'Progressivity' of a Flat Tax Family of Four
at Various Income Levels
(Flat Tax = 20 Per Cent)

Gross Income ($)	Taxable Income ($)	Actual Tax	Average Tax Rate (%)
36,000 and below	0	0	0.0
50,000	14,000	2,800	5.6
100,000	64,000	12,800	12.8
200,000	164,000	32,800	16.4
500,000	464,000	92,800	18.56
1,000,00	964,000	192,800	19.28

As income rises, the value of the $36,000 exemption proportionally shrinks, and the effective tax rate climbs.

Two rebuttals are offered to Gephardt. First, under the flat tax, half of all taxpayers (those earning $36,000 or lower for a family of four), would pay no income tax at all; those below $55,000 would pay at rates of 5.6 per cent (or lower) (see Table 1). This is better for low income households than Gephardt's 10 per cent rate. Even taxpayers with annual incomes up to $100,000—more that 90 per cent of all taxpayers—would pay only 12.8 per cent (or lower), barely higher than Gephardt's 10 per cent. For those who want 'progressivity', the flat tax offers more of it than Gephardt, even if progressivity is not its main intention.

The second argument is this: since the lower 50 per cent of income earners pay no income tax at all, any redistributive effects on who pays how much in taxes are confined within the top 50 per cent. In the US, as we have seen, 50 per cent of all household income begins at about $36,000. Moreover, households earning up to $55,000 are still paying only a small amount of income tax (5.6 per cent or less). The rationale for progressivity is supposed to be to relieve the poor. Is it worth it to fight over which portion of the income earners in the top 40 per cent pay a slightly higher (or lower) proportion than others? Does $55,000 per annum count as poor?

A newer argument is also relevant. My colleague Kevin Hassett is working on a paper that puts a number—a cost—on the preference for the current system over the flat tax. Even its opponents admit that the efficiencies of the flat tax would result in a five per cent gain in GDP. (More realistic estimates are twice that or more.) On a $9 trillion GDP, a five per cent gain is equivalent to about $450 billion. Thus, to resist the flat tax in order to keep the current complicated scheme comes at a cost of $450 billion. (The real cost, of course, could be significantly higher, as much as a trillion dollars per year or more.) Do those who value progressivity value it highly enough to renounce $450 billion or more in annual economic growth? Any progressivity that they do achieve will consist solely in rearranging the proportions of tax paid by the top 40 per cent of income earners. Do they really care that much whether the top five per cent, or the next 15 per cent, pay a slight proportion less (or more) than they are now paying? After all, under the proportional or flat tax, the bottom 50 per cent pay no income tax at all.

For completeness, I should also examine various proposals for a national sales tax or consumption tax, as a replacement for the current income tax and as an alternative to the proportional or flat tax. But that would excessively complicate an already long paper.[23]

Conclusion

These three modest public policy initiatives will not inaugurate the kingdom of God among men, but they will be at least small steps on the way to reducing the role of big government in our lives and to empowering individual citizens, their families, and their associations in civil society.

They are modest steps in the devolution from state to civil society that is likely to characterise the political and social history of the twenty-first century.

A friend of mine has christened this set of ideas 'universal family capitalism'. However, his proposal for naming this set of ideas might rub against the prejudices of Europe. Europe has spent more than 150 years denigrating capital. Too bad. Ordinary families are much helped by having it. Making a capital stock universal among families is a worthy aim.

Commentaries

The Future of the Welfare State

Anthony Giddens

WHAT is to become of the welfare state? Michael Novak is quite right to emphasise this as a basic question of political policy of our times, although he is hardly alone in doing so. Welfare reform is on the agenda almost everywhere. There are a variety of diagnoses about why this should be so, just as there are about the shape welfare institutions should best assume in the future.

In approaching Novak's views, a number of initial observations might be made. Perceptions of the welfare state in Europe tend to be quite different from the US, and reflect real differences in its role in the two contexts. In Europe, a whole generation has seen the welfare state as a springboard to social mobility and prosperity. The idea that welfare institutions inevitably dampen initiative or responsibility has to be treated with caution. In discussing 'the' welfare state, it is worth recognising the gulf between the American and the European experience—as well as the diversity of welfare systems that exist in European countries.

We should also beware of two forms of misplaced nostalgia, which I would call left and right nostalgias. Left nostalgia harks back to a golden age of the developed welfare state coupled to full employment—now threatened with being put into reverse. Things were never that rosy. As rightist critics say, the welfare state did and does create unaccountable bureaucracies, quite often profligate and inefficient. Some of the comments Novak makes seem to me ridiculous, such as 'the welfare state corrupts us ' (p. 8) or 'the peoples of the welfare state have once again become serfs'. But welfare dependency and welfare fraud are real and widespread in all forms of welfare state.

Right nostalgia, however, is just as misleading as its opposite. This is longing for a traditional family which never existed and for spontaneous forms of social solidarity that have somehow been corrupted by the state. Novak's article is suffused with this second sort of nostalgia. Big government is the enemy of the authentic family and of social order which somehow without its intervention would spontaneously well up from below. No 'think global, act local' here, just 'think local, act local'. Burke's talk of the little platoons is deployed as if they were a lost reality. Compared to the small-town society to which we are supposed to revert, the welfare state charts a path of destruction. It is blamed successively for 'a sterile and punitive redistributionism' (p. 2), 'destroying our human capital' (p. 6), penalising 'creativity and hard work' (p. 9)—and destroying family life, 'the most devastating piece of evidence in the case against the welfare state' (p. 10).

We won't have much chance of effectively reforming welfare institutions, in Europe or the US, if we accept such ideas, which are not exactly compelling. For authors on the right, the welfare state has become as much a bogeyman as 'capitalism' used to be for those on the left. Since the European countries have fuller welfare systems than the US, Europe is seen as in a hopeless economic situation. But this is not so.

Welfare states can redistribute income in two ways: across the life-cycle and between socioeconomic groups. Comparative evidence suggests they have been considerably more successful in the first area than in the second; but the European welfare states have been more effective in both respects than the US. Novak writes as though the US economy is prospering, whereas those of the European Union are not. However, an economy in which there are large numbers of working poor, and where the bottom 25 per cent have seen their incomes stagnate in real terms for the past twenty years, cannot be seen as an unalloyed success story. The US economy grew less strongly than some of the major Western European countries between 1988-1995. Even the picture as concerns unemployment is more complex than is often assumed. Stephen Nickell has shown that, over the period from 1983-1996, looking at OECD European countries, 30 per cent have in fact had lower unemployment rates than the United States.[1]

The notion that the welfare state undermines the family is an old chestnut of rightist critics, but not one to let pass. The society which has the highest rate of divorce, and one of the highest proportions of children born to unmarried mothers, the US, has the most weakly developed welfare institutions. There is in fact no clear correlation between welfare expenditure and levels of divorce or children born out of wedlock. In any case, the crisis of the family—and I see it as such—is much more complicated than Novak makes it seem. The more we learn from historians about traditional families, the more oppressive they often appear to have been; the expansion of children's rights and the increasing legal and economic equality of women with men are advances from which there can and should be no retreat. The crisis of the family is not one of disintegration, but of how to accommodate to a series of profound changes affecting it and surrounding institutions: marriage, sexuality, gender relations and the relation between home and work.

I don't disagree with the thesis that Tony Blair's election in 1997 confirms the failure of socialism as an economic system of management. Yet rather than marking the 'triumph of Margaret Thatcher' it confirms also the failure of Thatcherism, and neo-liberalism more generally. Neo-liberalism was an attempt to respond to the new conditions in which we live—to the impact of globalisation and intensifying global economic competition. It was deeply flawed, not least because of its paradoxical mix of economic libertarianism and moral traditionalism. Thatcherism wanted to modernise the economy but 'de-modernise' other areas, including the family—the same perverse position that Novak adopts too. In some other respects, Thatcherism was thoroughly at odds with the reforms Novak wishes to achieve. It was the enemy of devolution, since Mrs Thatcher drained power away from local councils and other bodies to the central state.

Responding to globalisation, and the cluster of other forces gathered around it, is the dominant agenda at the turn of the century. The issue is not, as Novak puts it, one of being optimistic or agitated about globalisation—supposedly the American versus the European view. Globalisation is not a single set of influences, but a complex set of structural transformations, affecting the economy, politics and culture. We have to understand these properly if we are to cope with and benefit from them. Globalisation is not only about the global marketplace and the expansion of the 'weightless economy'—the world information economy. It concerns the shifting role of the state itself and at the same time introduces many changes in everyday life, including those affecting the family. Globalisation pulls upwards, away from the nation-state—the state loses control of some sort of decision-making where it was previously more powerful. But it also pushes downwards, creating pressures towards greater local autonomy below the level of the state—globalising forces help promote the decentralisation of which Novak speaks. At the same time, globalisation squeezes sideways. It produces new regions and alliances which can cross-cut national borders—a phenomenon well-analysed by Keniche Ohmae.[2]

This complex of changes stands behind the dissolution of socialism and the obsolescence of social democracy. Social democracy in Europe has achieved far more than Novak would allow. But it is no longer a way to the future and the welfare state, in its diversity of forms, stands in need of a radical rethink. To be 'radical' here no longer means being on the left, because on this issue the left by and large has turned conservative. Yet nor does it mean just looking for ways to cut down on welfare expenditures. Social democracy has a great deal to be proud of. We should aim to preserve its achievements while recognising that existing welfare systems were oriented to a world that has largely disappeared.

What principles should guide reform of the welfare state? Allowing for many variations between national contexts, I would focus on the following:

1 Devolution of power and the idea of subsidiarity, as Novak says, are central to the restructuring of government and the welfare state. There is no way, however, that effective government can be achieved, or social integration fostered, through submerging the state in civil society. The reconstruction of government has to track the movement of globalisation, implying the 'upwards devolution' of power towards transnational agencies as well as new forms of regional government. The European Union should be understood today as both an expression of and a response to globalisation.

2 The development of economic and personal responsibility should indeed be a fundamental emphasis of welfare institutions. Welfare reform, as Tony Blair argues, should take this as a guiding theme. Where welfare dependency and the fatalism which can accompany it have become culturally entrenched, it should be the object of welfare institutions to foster renewed initiative and autonomy. Yet the principle of collective responsibility is equally important. Private provision, whether by individuals, families or business firms, can't wholly replace the responsibilities of the collectivity towards the individual.

3 The idea that public policy can somehow control family life is, I suppose, presumed in Novak's claim that the travails of the family are the unintended outcome of the welfare state. But in a democratic society neither government as such nor welfare systems can determine the evolution of family patterns. No one would dispute the need for strong families if this means family settings which are stable over the long-term, offer support and a measure of happiness for these involved in them, and protect the interests of children. The difficult issues today are deciding what types of relationship confer these benefits, and how they are to be reconciled with personal autonomy.

4 The issue of pensions reform needs a more radical approach than that suggested by Novak—one that addresses the changing position of older people in modern societies. Old age should be seen not as a problem but an opportunity, and the needs of the frail elderly distinguished from those of older people more generally. The category of 'pensioner' can create a culture of dependency as socially burdensome as any of the forms of welfare dependency found among younger groups. Privately-held pension funds however cannot do the job alone for several reasons.[3]

5 Welfare reform should aim to achieve a new balance of risk and security in people's lives. Willingness to take risks is a basic part of personal initiative and responsibility, as is risk assessment. Much of the welfare state is a form of collective insurance but, unlike the case of private insurance, debates about the welfare state have given little attention to the changing nature of risk. The post-war welfare state was built around a passive notion of risk—and a passive notion of security. If you fall ill, are disabled, get divorced or become unemployed, the welfare state will step in to protect you. We now live in much more active risk environments—an observation which stretches all the way from global markets through to family relations and health-care systems. Welfare systems need to contribute to the entrepreneurial spirit, encourage the resilience necessary to cope with a world of speeded-up change, but provide security when things go wrong. Welfare to work, the reform of tax systems and a range of other quite concrete policies can contribute to pursuing this ambition.

Serf No More

John Lloyd

MICHAEL Novak's style of argument is disconcerting. Social democracy is the enemy, so on it must be pinned the main guilt for *anomie*. Yet he cannot help observing that the leading society which is *not* social democratic, the United States, has a uniquely (among wealthy states) large crime problem. Is it better to have the moral hazard of people cheating the state by claiming they are sick when they are not, or the physical hazard of robbery with violence? Is there, perhaps, a trade-off between these two?

He slips into little parables to illustrate a general impression—like the parable of the busy barber of Italy who would not hire more help because of the bureaucracy. A sad tale. It wholly fails to explain why Italy's unemployment rate in the central and northern parts of the country is around three per cent (Italian unemployment is disastrously high in the south, which gives a high national figure); or why Italian cafés, shops, garages and offices—in the private sector—are so generously staffed; or why the Italian small and medium sized enterprise sector is so dynamic.

Europe must be paraded as mired in welfarism and social democracy; there must thus be no discussion of the European Union's largest project, monetary union—a project which will construct at the heart of the Union an institution and a set of rules which will force—already has forced—the participating member countries to apply the utmost rigour to their public expenditures. There must be no recognition that the bloated man of Europe, Italy, has, led by left-of centrists, hugely reduced the state expenditure, ended the era of automatic subsidies to state-owned or controlled industries and services, which it is privatising, and begun to restore some trust in a state debauched for decades by Christian Democrats who received the invariable blessing of the Vatican. (I put stress on Italy because the Prodi government, as Ralph Dahrendorf recently observed, is the un-noticed success story—in Novak's terms—of our times.) Nor must it be mentioned that Germany remains the most powerful industrial power in Europe. Nor that France's exports are increasing. Nor that France and Germany are both pulling strongly out of recession. The collapse on one side of the Atlantic must be presented as more-or-less total, the revival in the US as more-or-less unalloyed. The link between welfare and decline on the one hand and individualism and growth on the other must be asserted as being unbreakable.

This is a bad way to argue—the worse for forcing into absurdly constrained and distorted postures the phenomena Novak attempts to describe. Welfarism has gone hand in hand with rising levels of output, productivity, health, longevity, living space and, of course, income for most of the post-war period in all of the countries in which a welfare state has been in existence. To argue, with Irving Kristol (quoted by Novak), that: '[the] fully developed welfare state is a modern version of the feudal castle, guarded by moats and barriers, and offering security and shelter to the loyal population that gathers round it' (p. 9), grants the citizens of these states the status of serfs—a word which Novak flings about with abandon. Those of us born soon after the war to low-income families for whom a welfare state was a prop for caring for their ailing old and educating their ignorant young, as well as cushioning them from the harder things in life, are not about to accept serfdom's status. From that perspective, Novak's claim that social democracy destroys families is simply a bad taste joke.

No need for that, because we seem to have arrived at a relatively healthy political pass where policy can be examined with a deeper and more informed pragmatism than for much of this century. Social democrats, certainly in Germany, Britain, Italy and Holland but also increasingly elsewhere, are seeking to define the ground on which these pragmatic judgements can be made. Much of it is common to that occupied by Novak—to judge by the concerns which he raises towards the end of his essay. But they do not operate on a terrain in which social democratic institutions have been seen to fail utterly; on the contrary, they work within the constraints of a population attached, whether they are of right- or left-wing persuasion, to the institutions which social democratic government put in place. The British

National Health Service, the crowning domestic achievement of the post-war Labour government which remains among the most efficient in the world for money spent on services offered, retains such a grip on the affections of the electorate that no government can do other than pledge undying loyalty to it. (This does, indeed, often stifle thought about how to improve it.)

The new pragmatism thus operates among and on institutions and mechanisms which owe their origins to differing govern- ments of both left and right. No doubt that Margaret Thatcher was a pre-birth shaper of New Labour, as Novak says (but spoils by hyperbole: Thatcher's 'weaning of New Labour from... the enervating Nanny state' included *increased* state expenditure, largely because of the huge rise in the unemployed. There is not much more Nannyish expenditure than unemployment benefit); but Thatcher did not fundamentally change the post-war social democratic institutions, with the major exception of the national- ised industries. That task has been left to, and has been ac- cepted by, New Labour—just as it has been by the leftish Olive Tree coalition in Italy, the Dutch, Swedish and Danish social democrats and—in time, probably—by the French socialists and (if the party wins the election later this year) the German social democrats.

These groups bring different traditions and reflexes to the tasks of reform; more importantly, in the short term, they address differing landscapes. But all, most obviously New Labour, must now put by the ideological blinkers and examine policies for their effectivity, not for their (leftist) political correctness. Ideas like those of Novak's for portable pensions, medical savings accounts and proportional income taxes could be (are) part of the idea galaxy which open-minded governments will have to examine. It is, though, worth making the obvious point that such ideas, presented as they always are (as in Novak's essay) with the air of the plain man telling these stupid politicians what is obvious, are always fiendishly difficult to see through, precisely because the citizens of our societies are *not* serfs and object, individually, collectively and electorally, to radical reforms with which they do not agree or for which they have not been prepared. In the UK, the re-thinking of the welfare state associated with the Minister for Welfare Reform Frank Field has run into difficulties so great that both Field and his Secretary of State, Harriet Harman, were fired in an August reshuffle of the Cabinet. Field is the most engaged and best informed politician in the area; his political failure is an index of the fearsome difficulties of recasting a welfare system in a democracy.

Better to concentrate on general principles. Novak states the most important of these, the 'overarching aim', as, positively, residing in the need 'to raise up large numbers of strong, independent, creative, civic-minded and above all responsible citizens'; or, negatively, to 'reduce the dependency, passivity and irresponsibility now widespread in our societies' (p. 16). Who would not agree? I have said enough to make it plain that I believe that the welfare state has, and still can, further these aims rather than stand as the destroyer of them. But there is no disagreement that what we have needs fixing.

It seems true that:

• the rich will not tolerate paying higher, or in many cases not even the present, levels of taxation in order to raise the living standards of the poor. There is little fear of the working class, since it no longer appears threatening. There is some concern for the underclass, and that the state provide some sort of support for the aged, the sick, the demented and the helplessly poor. But there are tight limits, which seem to take their root in a perception that the welfare state is wasteful and that many of the poor are feckless.

• partly because of these constraints, the welfare state needs radical restructuring. Its commitments on health, social security and above all pensions cannot be sustained at present levels; the only direction possible is to shift responsibility for insurance for the tragedies and inevitabilities of life on to individuals and families.

• in many countries, but in the US and the UK in particular, large sums are spent on supporting single parents (almost invariably mothers); and large amounts of welfare are apparently being misdirected to fraudulent claims.

• on some (not all) measures, the social glue —however that is measured—is softening, and individuals and families are more prey to anomic behaviour. The organic communities of place or class are much weakened; and though new forms of community are evident or are being invented, they are still alien to many, especially those who are furthest down the education ladder and—usually—the income distribution ladder too. The Internet is a real community of interests, but it is inevitably exclusive of the poor and the ignorant.

The collapse of socialism, as Novak indicates, has removed the 'automatic pilot' mode of treating these problems. 'More social-ism'—by which was meant much higher taxes on the wealthier, public ownership, and state planning and powerful trade unions—is not a practical option. We also know that pure free marketry, in which welfare is reduced to allow those who cannot find jobs with a living wage to starve, does not answer the problem either—or, at least, seems not to, for no government, no matter how radically right, has tried it. Since we are not going back to (in the UK's case) a pre-1906 condition, then we are faced not with a choice between welfare and no welfare, but between different kinds.

I would put the principles of that somewhat differently from Novak. I agree we want individuals who are neither passive nor dependent; but these active, independent individuals will draw the possibility of being both from a framework which will, as far ahead as we can see, include a welfare statist element. And it should, for this not only ensures a minimum decency, but gives individuals, families and larger groups the sense of belonging to a wider community of interest than their own immediate rela-tives, friends and colleagues. The national—in Europe, increas-ingly the European—level is that at which decisions are made affecting everyday life, and thus it remains important for the civil society Novak wishes to strengthen that the citizen sees some provision which flows from his taxes, and which is open to all on roughly the same terms. Novak sees this as dependence. I think it is—to use a word inserted into the political lexicon by the former Labour leader Neil Kinnock—enabling. I am quite prepared to admit this is a subjective judgement. But when we use such concepts as passive, serf and dependent, we are usually being less than scientific.

The new leftist approach, in the US as elsewhere, concentrates on themes which in their general form certainly were and are those of the right also; the issue is with what content these general containers are filled. This approach gropes after a new practice of community—seeking to strengthen local communities above all, in part by holding people, or encouraging people to hold each other, to account for their everyday actions. It is true that people now can and sometimes do behave indecently (that is, short of criminally) to each other, and that this degrades social life; the answer is not necessarily less, but sometimes more, state, as we seek to re-build communal ties and reflexes through the media of local authorities and voluntary services. This will not be done spontaneously, at least at first—that, at any rate, appears to be the common perception of those who try.

An example from the UK. Both under this and the past governments, 'sink' or poor schools were singled out, given some extra resources, a new head teacher and close monitoring by the *national*, rather than the local, government (whose structures had often failed the school). The theory and the practice, insofar as there has been a track record to observe, is that the schools are brought back to some decent standard, and that the state can disengage. It appears that neither the locally elected councillors, the governors, *nor in some cases the parents*, were able to stop the slide into a degraded status; in most cases, the parents who did care had to appeal to the national government for redress, and for proper provision. Is this dependence? Or an active and rational response?

This illustrates another trope of the new leftists; responsibility. This government stresses the theme continually, unafraid to tread deep into what had been seen (not by all leftists) as right-wing territory. It is a fair point to make that this terrain has been best mapped by the right; but their charts are partial, with major gaps. Responsibility must have standards; must be prepared for; often requires training; at times benefits from outside agencies to raise its efficiency and its expectations. Who is accountable for what to whom is never a simple nor a fixed matter. It crucially depends on a sense of duty, which in turn is a product of many influences, of which care for one's own and one's family's behaviour is an important one. New Labour, especially the Prime Minister, lays much stress on duty, even more (at least rhetorically) than on rights; Tony Blair sees duty as the most important element in civil society, using the concept as it has been used by contemporary Christians.

It is a powerful, exemplary tool in his and in others' rhetoric (Jack Straw, the Home Secretary, is another enthusiast for it). It is or should be a powerful antidote to a hedonism which is asocial and uncivil in its effects—though, inevitably, those who are most asocial and uncivil are likely to locate themselves beyond the reach of rhetoric or example. But where new leftists would still differ from new rightists is that the former tend to import into the broad definition of duty a concern that the unequal positions of citizens be both made clear and in some way addressed—so that the duties they properly owe to society, to their families and their colleagues are not constantly much more onerous than those demanded from those who live within what J.K. Galbraith called the culture of contentment. Leftists would still contend that enabling, or, more contentiously, redistributive mechanisms must be set in place to assist the fulfilment of duties. This is still caricatured by the right as an attempt to blame society for the venalities and crimes of the poor or the deprived. It can be; it is not here, nor is it in current New Labour practice. It is an insistence that rights and duties necessarily and properly raise questions of access to material and non-material goods.

I said this last is contentious. It is contentious now not between left and right but within the left—another sign of how little it resembles the caricature Novak would still fit on it. We still, in fact, redistribute; marginal tax rates are higher for the better off; and Novak himself says that his common tax rate of twenty per cent is justified because it takes more in both percentage and absolute terms from the better off. The question is, should we assent to a greater redistribution than the relatively low level now operated—and that question remains, legitimately, open.

Novak's essay illuminates something of the paradoxical nature of our present debate. It is true, though it is over-simply true, that the left has moved onto right-wing territory. It is also true, however, that it seeks to pursue leftist goals from within it—goals such as greater equality of opportunity; a stricter accountability of both public authorities and private corporations to the public; a thicker and more diverse civil society. Much of this no longer has the ideological starkness of the past; the collapse of communism and the reconstruction of the practice of social democracy have seen to that. That seems to me to be a gain for the majority; yet it leaves the traditions and reflexes and practices of the left still with some object for their existence, some contribution to the common good still to be made—as it has been made, so remarkably, in the past.

The Traditions of Social Democracy

Paul Ormerod

MICHAEL Novak's essay is typical of the current misplaced triumphalism of the American right. The powerful and successful free-market American economy, with its low unemployment, is contrasted with the effete pinkos in Europe whose confidence and will to work are being sapped by the moral and financial burden of the welfare state.

Reality is rather more complex. True, the American economy has been by far the single most powerful and important one in the world for the best part of a century. And *average* living standards in the US remain higher than elsewhere in the industrialised world. The most systematic and thorough comparison of such matters across both time and countries was published by Angus Maddison in 1995.[1] He estimated that, in the mid-1990s, real per capita national income in the United States was around 25 per cent higher than in the main countries of continental Europe, such as France, (West) Germany and Italy.

But in terms of the rates of growth of the various economies, which are invoked by Novak as a fairer reflection of the underlying dynamism of an economy and society, the United States does not come out particularly well in international comparisons. Table 1 sets out the rates of growth of per capita national income, in real dollar terms, of America and the main European economies over a variety of time scales.

Each row of the table tells its own story. The first one, setting out growth rates over the course of the twentieth century, shows that the economies of continental Europe have grown slightly faster than the United States over the very long run. In other words, the American lead in living standards was already established as early as 1900. And it has been eroded rather than extended during the course of the century, despite the inexplicable attachment of degenerate Europeans to concepts of equity and the welfare state.

Table 1
Annual Rates of Growth of Real
Per Capita National Income

Period	United States	UK	France	Germany	Italy
1900-97	1.8	1.4	2.0	1.9	2.4
1950-97	2.0	2.0	2.7	3.3	3.5
1980-97	1.6	1.8	1.4	1.6	1.6

Source: Maddison for 1900-94 data and author's estimates 1995-7 from OECD national accounts
Note: income is measured in 1990 Geary-Khamis dollars

The second row shows the average annual growth since 1950, the period when the European welfare states have been at their strongest. Far from crippling the dynamism of the economies, the European welfare state has co-existed with extremely fast rates of growth over the course of half a century. Of course, the most rapid period of expansion was in the 1950s and 1960s when Europe was being re-equipped following the devastation of the war, so a period of catch up and rapid growth was only to be expected. But even so, it is not immediately apparent from this evidence that Europe has been undermined by welfarism.

Novak, of course, in common with many of the free-market right, argues that these adverse effects take time to register, citing a conversation with the Swedish economist Gunnar Myrdal by way of evidence. So the final row of Table 1 sets out the comparative growth rates from 1980, the date of President Reagan's election.[2] America has done rather better over this period, but its growth has still been no faster than that of West Germany and Italy, both of which retain deep attachments to the concept of the welfare state.

For much of the twentieth century, and certainly since 1945, successive European governments under a wide variety of political labels have consisted almost entirely of Novakian social democrats. According to Novak, this is an unequivocal recipe for economic failure: social democrats have 'concentrated more energy on helping the needy than on generating growth and opportunity'. They have given 'higher priority to redistribution than to incentives that reward achievement' (p. 15). This sounds fine as political rhetoric. But it is simply not consistent with the empirical evidence. Effete social democratic countries have grown just as fast as, and for the most part faster than, free-market America.

There is no sign at all in Novak's essay that he is aware of this simple but, from his perspective, devastating piece of evidence. Instead, we are offered long passages of assertions by the Pope, who is of course well known for his deep understanding of the economic theory of the dynamics of capitalism.

We are also treated to lengthy discussions of *predictions* that the European model of social democracy will no longer be valid in the future. Maybe it will and maybe it won't, but a prediction does *not* constitute evidence. Indeed, Novak himself is at pains to point out how the entirely unexpected can suddenly happen, citing the fall of the Shah of Iran and the collapse of the Berlin Wall as examples. Given the truly appalling record of skilled economic forecasters in predicting economic growth just *one* year into the future,[3] arguments based on predictions of longer-term growth rates are really of no value at all. The recent debacle in East Asia proves this point pretty conclusively. As recently as May 1997 the IMF was predicting seven per cent growth for the region in 1998, and the Asian model was eulogised as the way of the future.

All this does not mean that everything is well in European social democracy. The erosion of the traditional family is a matter of concern, not on moral grounds, but for functional reasons. As I have written with Bob Rowthorn of Cambridge,[4] the rise in divorce imposes costs on the rest of society which are not borne by the individuals directly involved, and it is therefore a matter of legitimate public policy to try to reverse this trend. However, without entering in detail into this debate here, it is very hard to see any connection across countries between the *overall* extent of the welfare state and the degree to which the traditional family has declined. Some of the biggest changes have taken place in countries at both extremes of attachment to the welfare state, namely the United States and Sweden. Both weak and strong welfare states have coincided with massive changes in family structures.

More particularly, and perhaps paradoxically given the evidence in Table 1, Europe has experienced a serious problem of inadequate growth over the past twenty years. As with family policy, this topic could merit an entire paper of its own, and the arguments made here are inevitably condensed.

There is a great deal to be admired about the United States. The confidence, resourcefulness and optimism of the American people are matters of historical record. Like any nation, the Americans are assailed from time to time by notions of self-doubt, but, in general, they usually have a brighter outlook on life than do Europeans. Europe, after all, unlike the United States, has twice been devastated this century by major wars, leaving many millions of dead. An acute awareness of such history is, for example, a crucial underpinning of the currently misguided project to unify Europe politically and economically. On a more utilitarian note, it is hard to see a company such as Microsoft emerging to world dominance so rapidly from Europe.[5]

But even given all this, at the level of the overall economy, productivity in the United States has grown at a slower—a slower, not a faster—rate than in social democratic Europe over the past twenty years or so. Since 1980, America and Europe have had very similar rates of *per capita* economic growth. In America, this has enabled unemployment to fall, whereas it has risen substantially in Europe. In other words, to keep unemployment from rising over time, Europe needs a faster rate of growth than the US, because Europe's underlying productivity growth is faster. More output growth is needed to create the same number of jobs.

It has become the conventional wisdom to ascribe this to 'rigidities' in European labour markets, in contrast to the 'flexible' American one. American Nobel prizewinner Robert Solow contested this view strongly in his November 1997 British Academy lecture,[6] arguing that, if anything, the American labour market can be thought of as having become less flexible in the 1980s, whereas no such evidence exists for France and Germany.

Whilst the conventional view has a certain amount of validity, it is considerably less important than the impact of inadequate growth rates on unemployment. Figure 1 plots the change in the annual average rate of unemployment in the pre- and post-oil shock periods against the change in the average rate of growth in a wide range of OECD economies.

Over the past twenty years or so, average GDP growth has fallen everywhere, and unemployment has risen. The chart shows that the two are very clearly connected. The greater the slow-down in growth, the higher the increase in the unemployment rate. For example, at one extreme we can see Spain in the top left hand bit of the chart. Reading down to the bottom axis shows that annual average GDP growth in Spain was over four percentage points less in the 1974-95 period than it was in 1960-73. And reading across the chart shows that Spanish unemployment rose by almost 12 percentage points. In contrast, at the other extreme, average growth in both the US and Norway fell by not much more than one percentage point, and the rise in unemployment in the two countries has averaged only two percentage points.

Figure 1
Change in Average Unemployment Rate and Economic Growth OECD Economies, 1974-95 on 1960-73

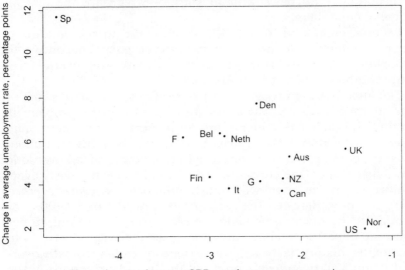

Change in annual average GDP growth rate, percentage points

Across the OECD, the slow-down in the rate of growth in the post-oil shock period accounts for 75 per cent of the increase in unemployment. There are three social democratic countries omitted from the chart—Austria, Portugal and Sweden—where the increase in unemployment was very *small* relative to the deterioration in the growth rate. And in Japan, similarly, the rise in unemployment was successfully contained.[7] The experience of the United States is entirely typical of the OECD as a whole. Given the fall in American growth since the mid-1970s, the change in unemployment is almost entirely explicable. American growth has fallen by less than almost every other OECD country, but it was much *lower* in the pre-oil period than elsewhere.

In short, a faster rate of growth is required to solve Europe's unemployment problem. But this will not be brought about by so-called Keynesian demand management policies.[8] Rather, longer-term, structural problems related to the profitability of European business need to be solved.

Profits in Europe have recovered from their low point around 1980, but they are still inadequate in two particular ways. First, the *average* share of profits of national income over this period was much less than it was in the 1960s and early 1970s. This can only serve to depress the buoyancy of long-term expectations—Keynes's 'animal spirits'—which are the driving force of capitalism.

Second, compared to America, profits tend to accumulate in more sheltered and protected industries, so the incentive to innovate and expand is less in Europe, at any given overall level of profitability, than it is in America.

The lack of an appropriate rate of profit in Europe has arisen for complex reasons, but a substantial part of the problem is entirely self-inflicted. Preparations for monetary union, stretching back to the initial Exchange Rate Mechanism (ERM) almost twenty years ago, have involved tight monetary policies over long periods of time. One consequence of this has been grossly over-valued exchange rates, which have only been partially reversed very recently. Between the early 1980s and the mid-1990s, for example, the mark appreciated in real terms by around 35 per cent against the dollar. And one lesson we can learn from economic history is that long periods of exchange rate over-valuation lead to squeezes on profitability and reductions in the longer-term rate of growth.

In short, different varieties of capitalism each have their own particular strengths and weaknesses, and all appear to be perfectly viable systems. There is nothing unique about the current situation to lead one to believe that the social democratic model is no longer sustainable. Technological innovation wiping out entire occupations and industries is not at all new. Indeed, it is precisely the ability to encourage such innovation on a persistent basis which distinguishes capitalism from all other forms of economic organisation in the history of the world. On many criteria the period before the First World War represented a more complete expression of globalisation than does our present era, and it was precisely during that time that the first foundations of the modern welfare state were laid.

Novak, in common with many right-wing Americans, fails to understand that European social democracy is now, and always has been in practice, just another species of the broad genus, capitalism. Its rhetoric, its institutions and its approach to many problems are different to the tooth-and-claw capitalism preached by many Republicans, but at heart it has a deep commitment to the fundamental conditions required for the operation of a capitalist economy. Most importantly, the existence of private property rights, principally over innovations and the stream of profits associated with them, and the rule of law is required.

For most of the twentieth century, social democrats have seen the state and state activity as instruments of progress. The first century or so of industrial capitalism was associated with lifestyles for the working class which can at best be described as grim. From Friedrich Engels' 1844 *Condition of the Working Class in England* to Robert Tressell's 1907 *Ragged Trousered Philanthropists*, a whole series of classic pamphlets and novels graphically related the day-to-day struggle for existence of the bulk of the population, often contrasted sharply with the opulent living of the fortunate few.

The state came to be regarded as the mechanism by which matters would be improved, in messianic literature by the suppression and overthrow of the capitalist mode of production. On a more practical basis, the state was seen as way of regulating affairs to make life that bit more tolerable, by, for example, limiting the working day ('A ten hour day for children! Good God, what do these socialists think they are playing at? I can't even send my boys up the chimney any more.'), permitting labour to organise, and by introducing the rudiments of the welfare state.

But in a wider historical context, the radical tradition had an entirely different attitude towards the state, hating and fearing it as an instrument of oppression. The Levellers and Diggers of the English Revolution had as little time for Cromwell and his state as he had for them. Such attitudes survived for a long period of time, and many of the early defensive responses by the working class to capitalism, surviving well into the twentieth century, reflected this tradition. Workers organised mutual assistance for health, provision for old age and unemployment, and even

education on a self-help basis, often in parallel with and aug-
menting similar provisions by the state.

The current debate amongst social democrats about the
appropriate role for the state can really be seen as resurrecting
this old, radical tradition. For a relatively brief period of time, the
state *was*, unequivocally, an instrument of progress. As even
Novak admits the welfare state is compatible with respect for
human rights, unprecedented levels of prosperity, a significant
increase in longevity and quality of life for the elderly (p. 13).

But it is foolish to believe that only the state can continue to
advance society, an attitude of mind which, sadly, does persist
amongst many members of the European left and which lays
them open to intemperate Novak-like attacks. To take just one
example, the British local authorities have been successfully
colonised by large numbers of the middle class. Whatever
judgement one might wish to pass on their overall intellectual
abilities, they have certainly shown a frightening ability to boost
their own numbers and to regrade and promote themselves to
ever higher salaries, whilst at the same time presiding over
deteriorating services to the local citizenry because of the 'cuts'.
In a related area, it has recently been deemed necessary to form
a quality assessment unit to monitor the output of the Training
and Enterprise Councils. This is one area where the market
might have been safely left to make its own decision, with local
companies as the arbitrators of whether or not to pay for TEC
services. But, nevertheless, the chief executive of the new unit
will soon have two brand new deputies, 20 full-time staff and,
amazingly, no less than 500 part-time employees. O Gosplan,
thou shouldst be living at this hour!

Ironically, given his attachment to the free market, Novak takes
a far too pessimistic view of the strength and resilience of
capitalism. It is the only type of economic system in human
history which has been able to generate consistent growth over
very long periods of time. The planned economies of the Soviet
bloc did appear to offer a challenge, so much so that as late as
the 1960s many Americans feared they would be overtaken
economically by the Soviet Union, but they proved unable to
adapt beyond the initial phases of industrialisation and capital
accumulation.

The success of capitalism has come about against a background of an enormously wide variety of political regimes and

institutions. Even liberal democracy itself does not appear to be a necessary condition for capitalism to take root and prosper, judging by the circumstances under which Japan, for example, first developed, or by the various experiences of Germany in the first half of this century and of East Asian countries in more recent decades.

Yet the closing years of the twentieth century see a group of Western nations, all rich beyond the imagination of previous societies, at broadly similar levels of income per head, having experienced broadly similar rates of economic growth for more than a hundred years.

Paradoxically, it is the capitalist mode of production and not the concept of social democracy which has proved to be the most important instrument of social justice. It has been the ability of capitalism to generate slow but steady growth which has raised personal living standards, has made the welfare state affordable, and which has liberated many millions of people from lives of unremitting toil and drudgery. In the sixty years which separated the writings of Engels and Tressell, for example, real wages in Britain approximately doubled. The conditions facing Tressell's Edwardian housepainters were much worse than anything we see today, but through economic growth they were much better than those endured by their counterparts in the 1840s.

The effect of overtly social democratic programmes designed to promote social justice has been of a second order of importance compared to the impact of economic growth. And, without doubt, many such schemes have had entirely unexpected, adverse consequences. But such outcomes are inevitable in the process of attempting to manage systems of the extreme complexity of modern economics and societies. Indeed, the enthusiasts for the free market in the United States in the 1980s could hardly have intended as an outcome the current position in Manhattan, where at the same time as many celebrate bonuses of millions of dollars, and regard a mere single million as no more than 'tip' money, thousands of their compatriots queue at the soup kitchens.

In many ways, the Adam Smith not just of the *Wealth of Nations* but of the *Theory of Moral Sentiment* was one of the first social democrats of the modern era. Smith emphasised the moral climate in which the economy and society function, and an important role of the state was precisely to assume powers to support that framework. One of his special concerns, for example, was the impact of the division of labour on the quality of life of the labouring poor. This principle of organisation brought enormous benefits in material terms, but rendered many individuals 'not only incapable of relishing or bearing a part in any rational conversation, but of conceiving any generous, noble or tender sentiment'. For Smith, the state had the very important role of tackling this problem by providing a level of education sufficient to render every citizen capable of exercising an appropriate level of intellectual and social 'virtue'.

It is ludicrous to argue that, at a time of unprecedented wealth and prosperity, the nations of the West cannot afford the welfare state, just as it is naive to remain fixated with a model of progress which happened to be valid at the turn of the last century. But the guiding principles of social democracy, whatever their practical manifestation, remain just as valid now as they were in the time of Adam Smith. And the social democratic view of human beings operating within a society and of having obligations to each other has been and remains entirely compatible with the functioning of a market-based and successful economy.

Rejoinder: Considerable Common Ground

Michael Novak

PERMIT me, first off, to apologise for those of my remarks that inflamed passions and awakened defensiveness. The commentators are to be congratulated for passing over those as swiftly as possible and discovering considerable common ground. Both in the United States and in Britain we face sufficiently grave problems over the next twenty years that we will each need cooperative and practical help, without needless misunderstandings.

In this reply, therefore, I shall try to emphasise the common ground marked out between these three good critics and myself, and put in second place—but not neglect—our remaining differences. I particularly liked Paul Ormerod's chiding me, for example, that I take 'a far too pessimistic view of the strength and resilience of capitalism' (p. 44). I hold the same view of Adam Smith as he does, and am fond of quoting the conclusion of many Smith scholars, to the effect that Smith himself outlined at least a score of different types of interventions that the state ought to make to improve the social order. Indeed, reading Smith reinforced my original intuition, many years ago, that the free society cannot be understood as a free economy alone, since the free economy itself depends in significant measure upon its surrounding polity and culture.

In the United States, however, when I have argued that social democracy is a variant of democratic capitalism—that the two are species of one genus, perhaps even complementary cousins—I have more often than not been rebuked by social democrats. Perhaps the ideological divisions in Britain are deeper and clearer, so that pragmatic adjustment is less threatening, whereas in the US those sufficiently far on the left to call themselves social democrats (instead of, simply, democrats or even liberals) feel passionately the need not be recognised as capitalists of any stripe.

In any case, Paul Ormerod states my own conviction so well that he takes my breath away: 'Paradoxically, it is the capitalist mode of production and not the concept of social democracy which has proved to be the most important instrument of social justice. It has been the ability of capitalism to generate slow but steady growth which has raised personal living standards, has made the welfare state affordable, and which has liberated many millions of people from lives of unremitting toil and drudgery'. This is an uncommonly generous assessment, coming from a social democrat, and so is the one he adds a paragraph later: 'The effect of overtly social democratic programmes designed to promote social justice has been of a second order of importance compared to the impact of economic growth' (p. 45).

When I myself reached judgments such as these, after reviewing some of the evidence in economic and social history (not my primary fields), I found myself attacked as a 'neo-conservative', an ascription that I spent some years resisting, before surrendering to what I could not prevent. If it is possible in Britain to be a social democrat and also to hold such views as Ormerod's (as plainly it is), then we are much closer to reading music from the same sheets than we were just a decade or two ago.

Social Democracy as Faith

Not that there are not differences between social democrats and what I have been calling democratic capitalists. When Ormerod cites Adam Smith as one among our models, I am with him. But when, in the next breath, he writes about 'the social democratic view of human beings', this sounds to me more like a religion—a view of man—than like social policy. I like philosophical and religious discussions very much and would be happy to read more about this philosophical 'view'.[1] Perhaps that is the element that gives social democracy a sort of transcendence, beyond the reach of any particular empirical test—a vision that leaves enormous historical room for trial and error, beginnings and revisions, false starts and new directions. Social democrats seldom have to say they were wrong; confident in good intentions, they simply pivot in a new direction. At least, so it seems. A discussion of the relation between the 'view' and the practice would be very welcome.

By contrast, democratic capitalism may be less poetic.[2] A democratic capitalist is one who, from one or other of many different philosophical visions or religious backgrounds, is committed to three interdependent sets of institutions or systems: *a democratic polity* (limited government under the rule of law, protection of rights, checks and balances, etc.); *a capitalist economy* (with more stress on enterprise and invention than on the three pre-capitalist features: markets, private property, and accumulation); and *a culture that nourishes the habits*, social and individual, required by free societies.

In this respect, democratic capitalism is rather less of a faith than social democracy. The term itself does not designate 'a view of human beings' in the way that social democracy seems to. Rather, it designates a set of institutions that appear from trial and error to be necessary for a society that wishes to become, and to remain, free. (Perhaps it would be better to say that it designates a range of institutions, since democratic capitalism permits of a wide variety of quite different formations and structures; no two democratic capitalist systems seem to be the same.) Peter Berger has shown that a capitalist economy seems to be a necessary condition for democracy—necessary but not sufficient—but the reverse, as Paul Ormerod comments, is not true.[3]

Still, if I were to designate one theme that seems to differentiate social democrats from democratic capitalists, that theme would be the meaning and importance each attaches to equality. I must leave it to social democrats to spell out what they mean by equality, and what limits they would assign to it. For my part, let me state my own reservations. Obviously, 'equal justice under the law', 'equality of status' (no privilege of birth or station), and 'equal opportunity' (meaning open and abundant opportunities for those at the bottom) are necessary pre-requisites of a free and good society. When Abraham Lincoln, in the context of a war to emancipate the slaves, speaks at Gettysburg of 'a nation conceived in liberty, and dedicated to the proposition that all men are created equal', he gives voice to both religious and republican beliefs that we all share. These ideals are not simply given in history; they have to be realised at the cost of blood and tears. Plainly, then, there are senses in which equality is a proper, beautiful, and longed-for ideal. But there are also dangers to the idea, and warnings to be heeded.

Tocqueville has warned that, like a contradiction at the heart of democracy, the idea of equality, propelled by the power of

majorities, tends to smother the idea of liberty. Madison referred
to a 'wicked rage' for equality. In short, experience teaches that
a great many sins are committed in the name of equality. As a
social passion, envy is even more destructive than hatred, since
everyone recognises that hatred is evil, while envy seldom goes
under its own name, preferring to travel under the disguise of
more noble names, including equality and fairness. How can one
tell the difference between a genuine passion for equality and
envy?

For myself, a fairly useful rule of thumb runs as follows: to try
to raise the living conditions of the poor has a higher moral
status than to try to bring down the rich. The first impulse is
likely to spring from creative generosity and an admirable love for
equality; the latter, to spring from envy, anger and destructive-
ness. Sometimes, of course, the rich conduct themselves with
cruel injustice, and such contemptuous disregard for the
condition of the poor, that the cry of vengeance rises in the throat
as if it were the voice of justice itself. In some cases, it might be.
Still, it is all too easy, especially in societies with the historical
background of hereditary divisions by class, to imagine that
wealth earned through business is the cause of the poverty of the
poor, and that in capitalist societies 'being rich' is like being born
a hereditary baron.

Many of those who have become rich through business were
born poor; many are anything but aristocratic. More than that,
the businesses they have created also help others to rise from
poverty. Inequality is less a problem than a natural condition,
but a lack of decent sustenance commensurate with human
dignity *is* a human problem and within our power to alleviate.
The latter is more likely to be solved by the creation of more
business opportunities for those at every level, especially the
poor, than by redistribution. Education for low-income youths is
also important, so that they can take advantage of opportunities.

The social problem, further, is not that there are too many
persons creating new industries, new products, new services,
new wealth, and new jobs. We need more of the kind of enterprise
such persons show, not less, and at every social level.

All three of my critics, in different ways, concur that the needs
of the poor cannot be fully met by 'redistribution' from the rich.
In addition, we need to create conditions so that considerably
more of the poor in each of our own societies can, if they want to,

learn the skills and find the means to move out of poverty as in the last three generations many already have. Some of the institutions and programmes of the welfare state have contributed to this success. On the other hand, some programmes seem to be spinning their wheels and wasting resources; and some appear to be doing positive harm. Without exception, my critics concur that the tasks undertaken by the welfare state since 1945 need to be reconsidered and re-imagined, in the light of lessons learned, new conditions, and new needs.

Paul Ormerod makes much, as well he should, of the tables showing annual rates of growth between 1900 and 1997 in the United States and several key nations of Europe. I found these numbers counter-intuitive at points, but since I am not an economist by training I have no recourse but provisionally to accept them. Ormerod has himself added some necessary brackets: the American standard of living was already higher in 1900. Thus, even though annual growth rates in several European nations have on the whole been higher—especially in the years following the devastation wrought by World War II—relative position has remained fairly constant. I would only add that in a continental-sized economy like that of the United States, after a certain point increments in the growth rate become harder to maintain and, nonetheless, each small measure of growth, on the far larger base, means substantially larger wealth for the nation as a whole. Two per cent annual growth in a $7 trillion economy is $140 billion per year—one-tenth of the entire GDP of Germany.

Still, Ormerod's main point is that societies more social democratic than the US have had annual growth rates superior to that of the US, so I should be careful to give them due credit. I should also be careful not to link innovation solely to the US. In one respect, though, I think I am right about this: the US has so strong a culture of invention, discovery, and risk-taking and, just as important, so widespread a habit of capital investment in new ventures, that it is far easier for new technologies to get launched. Almost half the venture capital of the world is invested in the United States, and a much higher proportion of that in entirely new ventures (rather than in established firms) than in any other country. This habit has costs, of course, since Schumpeter's 'creative destruction' is a two-edged sword.

Ormerod also brings to light three other points that support my analysis. European businesses face more serious obstacles to profitability than American firms. Second, 'the incentive to innovate and expand is less in Europe'. Third, to keep full employment, Europeans need higher rates of job growth than the US. Ormerod attributes this need to higher productivity gains in Europe. Perhaps so, but that claim seems suspect to this non-economist. In Italy, as John Lloyd notes, overstaffing even in private firms is endemic; but so, too, is the hidden economy of the second job. In addition, European work rules seem to American firms woefully inefficient; for American managers, they take some time getting used to.

Dependency and Pre-moral Conduct

It is easy to agree with John Lloyd that the aims of Prime Minister Prodi in setting the left in Italy on a new course are much to be applauded. Yet it seems a little early to claim a victory. Many crises lurk just ahead. And many on the Italian left still resist change. Too many well-educated, bright young Italians must leave behind the mild climate and good food of Italy to find jobs abroad. Italy has had no Thatcher or Reagan—or even a large party likely to produce one. If it is true that only parties of the left can reform the welfare state, it is also true that a prolonged scare from a centre-right party of growth and opportunity wonderfully concentrates the social democratic mind.

Like good social scientists, all my commentators are suspicious of parables and anecdotes, but I find the few little stories they place in their own accounts very helpful. If I may generalise this observation, the study of statistical tables in cross-cultural comparisons carries understanding only so far; a foreigner needs a little help in getting a feel for a way of life from the inside, and this a good parable can partly convey.[4] Thus, when John Lloyd writes that: 'Those of us born soon after the war to low-income families for whom a welfare state was a prop for caring for their ailing old and educating their ignorant young, as well as cushioning them from the harder things in life...' (p. 31) he wrests recognition and sympathy from me, and reminds me of my own youth. He makes plain that social democracy and welfare are not merely abstractions, but part of the texture of his life and memory and hope.

Meanwhile, Lloyd is generous in drawing attention to the points on which we agree, both about new proposals to be studied seriously (the proportional tax, portable pensions, medical savings accounts) and about certain lessons learned from the experience of the past forty years (that there are limits to taxation; that pensions cannot be sustained at current levels; that the welfare state needs radical restructuring; that large amounts of welfare appear to be being misdirected; and that the social texture of society is wearing thin and rupturing).

Again, Lloyd concedes that the 'automatic' solution of the left in the past no longer works—the sort of 'more socialism' that meant 'much higher taxes on the wealthier, public ownership, state planning, and powerful trade unions'. In return, I freely concede to him that the free market alone is not enough, and that nowadays some sort of welfare system is almost always needed. Ronald Reagan, it is sometimes said, legitimated the welfare state for conservatives—a reformed and limited welfare state, no doubt, but not abandoned. Lloyd is right: '[W]e are faced not with a choice between welfare and no welfare, but between different kinds' (p. 34).

So far as they go, I can agree with nearly all the main points of Lloyd's last ten or twelve paragraphs, although it is probably true that if he went into more detail our divergences would leap into sight. I benefited by his parable on school reform, for example, and tend to agree that the principle of subsidiarity works in both directions—sometimes the intervention of the higher body, sometimes the workings of the local body, better serve the good. The trick is to prevent the one from crippling the other.

Further, I do not hold, as he charges, that every form of assistance from the state creates dependency, or even that every form of dependency is wrong. When I was young, I depended on my parents, and when I am old I will depend (I hope not too weightily) on my children, along with social security. For many goods, I depend on government and many other institutions, from scholarships and loans to subsidised goods or services. Some forms of dependence are natural, healthy and good; the stance of perfect independence is usually an affectation and a self-deception.

Discussions of 'dependency' in the context of welfare, however, point to something else: the failure by a small proportion (but sizable number) of healthy grown adults to meet the normal responsibilities of persons of their station. These mostly young people suffer from their own lack of social development; their fault seems far less 'moral' than 'pre-moral'—their conduct hardly rises to the level of the moral and the deliberate. It is as if a significant portion of the population is being allowed to, or induced to, live in a kind of pre-moral suspended animation. (This is what I meant by 'serfdom'. In America, it occurs almost precisely in coincidence with post-1964 welfare.)

'Dependency' means here that their children cannot count on them; and neither can their parents or others who might need their help. Further, these unfortunate ones shirk personal responsibility, fail to take advantage of opportunities (to finish school, for example), and turn habitually to the public purse and the public rescue services (to clean up the messes they some-times make), without making any effort to contribute to the public need in return. Such persons seem all taking and no giving. In the large picture, they are not many but, added all together, their costs to the public purse are many, and their contributions to public disorders and what social scientists have named 'social pathologies' are disproportionately high.[5]

In a second category are those recipients of public bene-fits—young and healthy and, in normal times, expected to be able to carry their own weight—who may at first be helped, rescued even, by welfare, but then seem to become 'addicted' to it, and rest in it as a way of life, causing thereby measurable damage to themselves and their own children. It does not seem to be the case that welfare can do only good to people. Among recent immigrants to the United States, word circulates that they should avoid welfare at all costs, that it is a 'honey pot', and that once trapped in it they may find it difficult to get out.

Since in the last two decades the US has received more immigrants than in any earlier decades but two, the public as a whole has learned to distinguish clearly between poverty (shared by nearly all immigrants for a time) that is temporary, and a dependency that cuts far deeper into observable behaviour. Monetarily, one family (on welfare or not) may be poorer but on a path toward exiting from poverty. Its financially better off neighbour may be trapped in personal behaviours (drugs, alcohol, avoidance of work, having children out of wedlock, dropping out of school, criminal behaviours) highly predictive of further sufferings to come.

Another example: some seventy per cent of recently separated or divorced women who turn to welfare for assistance at the moment of crisis find employment and are off welfare within two years. Such women tend to be older and to have already acquired useful skills. In such cases, welfare is working as it was intended to work—extending a hand where it was needed. By contrast, younger and less prepared women, especially if they have had children but never married, are far more likely to have many and long episodes of welfare; and the prognosis for the health, education, and well-being of their children is bleak. Here the danger of welfare actually harming those it is intended to help is more acute.

The new welfare reforms of 1996 are aimed at breaking 'the cycle of dependency' described in such examples, while continuing to provide a safety net for those thrown off balance by temporary misfortune. Those who are ill or disabled or in other ways permanently in need will, of course, be supported for as long as necessary. We await anxiously the results, intended and unintended, of these new reforms, which went into effect only in the fall of 1997.

Lloyd's closing paragraphs show that on matters such as 'duty', 'responsibility', and 'care for one's own and one's family's behaviour', he is 'unafraid to tread deep into what had been seen (not by all leftists) as right-wing territory' (p. 35). The degree of new consensus on such matters is well worth celebrating, and I congratulate him for bringing it to our attention. Still, Lloyd signals that some of the differences between left and right persist, at least as tendencies; for example, the left's persistent concern, as mentioned above, with inequalities (a concern partly lovely, partly dangerous); with generating a sense of 'belonging' (in this, the left is more like a church than the right); and with imagining the right as always blaming the lot of the poor on 'the venalities and crimes of the poor or the deprived'.

By contrast, I would emphasise these points: often the poor can be helped by well-designed welfare programmes, in health care and education particularly, but also with respect to food and housing and even income supplements. One does not have to be a social democrat to work for these. And one does not have to do such work for the sake of 'equality', either, but rather in the name of bringing everybody up to a basic dignity and decent chance, for the good of society as a whole. Who knows what talent a poor lad may shelter within? Most of my neo-conservative friends were once, like Lloyd, poor lads and benefited from welfare. Such welfare, at least in America, was usually of a better design than that of the post-1964 'War on Poverty'.

Who Are The Poor?

About Anthony Giddens' good criticisms I need to say less, partly because many of his points have already been covered, and partly because so much of his piece is devoted to an elegant summary of points of consensus. His last paragraph, in particular, is a jewel, and I wish it had been my own. I like, too, his second paragraph on the difference in perceptions of the welfare state, as between Europe and America. The 'gulf' is as wide as he says—but recent movements of reflection on both sides of the Atlantic have, I think, as this symposium surprisingly shows, brought us much closer together.

When I wrote one of the phrases that Giddens finds 'ridiculous', *viz.*, that 'the welfare state corrupts us', perhaps another anecdote or two will bring to light the perception I intended to convey. In the US, a young professor is interviewed for a job; he is told by the dean that he will certainly get the job, and should not be dismayed by continued interviewing because the department will have to make an 'affirmative action' report recording that they had gone through all the required motions with other candidates. The same professor interviews at another university, and is told that the job simply must go to a minority or a woman, but that if he goes through with the interview it will look good on their records, so he is welcome to show up.

Again, in the 1960s a Harvard graduate student who accepted welfare benefits would have been shamed—such benefits as were then available were not intended for Harvard students. Today, it is not uncommon to meet young people—even university students—who work for a year or so, then collect unemployment or other benefits while taking time off for a 'break' in the mountains. The new attitude is quite different; the benefits are there for the taking.

Again, to claim certain allowances for disabilities, one needs a note from a doctor, but it is a hard-hearted doctor who will not be accommodating. On automobile, medical and other forms of insurance, padding is common. Something for nothing is pervasively corrupting, and I expected to be criticised for generalising the obvious. Nonetheless, Giddens himself immediately conceded the point I was reaching for: 'But welfare dependency and welfare fraud are real and widespread in all forms of welfare state'. I have long noted that when people on the left are about to make a point that sounds like a point of the right, they often first prove their bona fides to their friends on the left by jabbing a rightist.

Professor Giddens alleges that in America 'there are large numbers of working poor' and that 'the bottom 25 per cent have seen their incomes stagnate in real terms for the past twenty years'. I know that such sentences have become part of the conventionally reported picture, but there is much that tells against that picture. Two-thirds of the householders among the poor are women, half of them widows and the other half largely mothers of small children, fathers absent. Only a small proportion of these women are working full-time year round, if at all. The composition of the poor, in short, is no longer comparable to what it was fifty, or even thirty, years ago. The number of male householders, married, working full time, and still poor is now quite small, compared to then. The proportion of all the poor working full time year-round in 1996 was certainly not 'large'; it was 2.3 per cent.[6]

Further, the bottom 25 per cent would include all households with earnings of approximately $22,000 or less (1996). Most calculations of earnings during the past twenty years suffer from two deficiencies; first, they fail to count benefits, especially health benefits, whose costs to employers and value to employees in the past two decades have risen far faster than wages. Much labour union bargaining in recent years has accordingly been for benefits rather than wages.

Second, the calculator by which inflation, and hence real income, is measured has been widely recognised as out of sync with changing realities, thus overstating inflation by more than one per cent a year. Combined, these two deficiencies help to explain why the widely reported stagnation seems not to match what one sees with one's eyes.

Nonetheless, as Giddens says, this so-called golden age of the US economy is not an 'unalloyed success'. The severe bout of double-digit inflation for three years during 1979-1981 so deeply undercut real wages, especially of those on fixed incomes, that it took more than a decade of steady real growth merely to recoup the loss (a loss of nearly 50 per cent of purchasing power). This is what most hurt those at the bottom, those on fixed incomes most of all. (By contrast, the too-generous inflation measure boosted the incomes of those on social security, which are indexed thereto, more than probably was due.)

I certainly agree with the distinctions Giddens introduces concerning the family, as well as his warnings against nostalgia. But nostalgia is not my point about the family; I am not here arguing for traditional family values. (Neither would I be as certain as Giddens that in today's more 'progressive' world, family violence is less than in the past.) Rather, I am pointing out the heavy costs to the public of such recent social changes as widespread divorce, separation, births out of wedlock, and teenage pregnancy. In the United States, the fastest growing segment of the poor has been the father-absent mother with children. (This description, while attempting a suitable neutrality, suggests a growing irresponsibility and delinquency on the part of the male, not the female, sex.)

This subject is too delicate and complex to discuss as briefly as we must here; permit me to refer the reader to the study I mentioned in the introduction to my paper. The prognosis for a substantial proportion of the children born to father-absent households is not as favourable to public well-being, or as inexpensive for the public purse, as is the prognosis for the children of the intact husband/wife family. Whatever the relative moral merits of the two arrangements, the public policy preference is becoming clearer to all who examine the record.

Giddens is hard but fair regarding several of my formulations. He rightly points out (as I ought to have) the great achievements of social democracy, face-to-face with the ruins left by World War II, and the great European 'miracle' of that era. But when he writes now of our new time, of 'the dissolution of socialism and the obsolescence of social democracy', and when he lists his five principles to guide the acutely necessary reforms of the welfare state, he states in a masterly way what I was merely groping for. I can but agree with his five principles. They track reasonably well with those I fumbled to get at.

In brief, the commentators put in words what it was necessary for someone to say, and did so rather better than I did. Further, on many points, they also tried to move left and right closer to a practical consensus. They have given us a potentially more fruitful circle of debate than we have had for some decades. They deserve thanks on both sides of the Atlantic.

Notes

Michael Novak

1. Tocqueville, A. de., *Democracy in America*, (1835) translated by Lawrence, G., Meyer, J.P. (ed.), New York: Anchor Books, 1969, Vol. II, Part IV, Ch. 6, p. 692.

2. A useful conspectus of the dimensions of the coming welfare crisis, in its demographic and fiscal dimensions, is proffered in a special issue of *The American Enterprise*, 'Fixing Social Security', January/February 1997, p. 6.

3. *The Times Literary Supplement*, 9 May 1997.

4. Bork, R., *Slouching Toward Gomorrah*, New York: HarperCollins, 1996. See also William Bennett's *Index of Leading Cultural Indicators: Facts and Figures on the State of American Society*, New York: Simon & Schuster, 1994.

5. Tocqueville, *op. cit.*, pp. 691-692.

6. Walter, M. and Abbott, S.J. (ed.), *Gaudium et Spes*, #69, *The Documents of Vatican II*, Piscataway, NJ: New Century Publishers, 1966.

7. In Britain, see Green, D., *Reinventing Civil Society*, London: IEA, 1993, and Harris R. and Seldon, A., *Welfare Without the State*, London: IEA, 1987; in the US see Olasky, M., *The Tragedy of American Compassion*, Wheaton, Ill: Crossway Books, 1992.

8. Berger, P.L. and Neuhaus, R.J., *To Empower People: From State to Civil Society*, 20th anniversary edition by Michael Novak, Washington, DC: AEI Press, 1996.

9. 'The Spiritual Crisis of the Welfare State', *Wall Street Journal*, 3 February, 1997.

10. *Centesimus Annus*, sect. 48.

11. Over 50 per cent of all children born in Sweden are born out of wedlock compared with about 31 per cent in the United States. This difference is due in large part to the fact that 25 per cent of all couples in Sweden are living in consensual unions, compared with about five per cent in the US However, the divorce rate in Sweden is still surprisingly high—36 per cent compared with 42 per cent in the US. See Popenoe, D., 'Family Decline in the Swedish Welfare State', *The Public Interest*, Winter 1991, pp. 66-67. For further statistics on the United States, see *Report to Congress on Out-of-Wedlock Childbearing*, Washington, DC: Dept. of Health and Human Services, 1995. On Great Britain, whose illegitimacy rate has reached over 30 per cent, see Murray, C. *et al*, *Charles Murray and the Underclass: The Developing Debate*, London: IEA Health and Welfare Unit, 1996.

12. See Novak, M. (ed.), *The New Consensus on Family and Welfare*, Lanham, MD: UPA, Inc., 1987, pp. 29-31.

13 *Ibid.*, pp. 19, 58-70, 125.

14 *Ibid.*, pp. 5, 13-16, 98-99.

15 *Ibid*, pp. 98-119.

16 Tocqueville, *op. cit.,* pp. 189-95, 513-17.

17 For examples of the ways in which centralised governmental regulations and administrative rulings now stifle local initiatives, see the essays by Green, D., Horowitz, M. and Olasky, M., in *To Empower People: From State to Civil Society, op. cit.*

18 Pear, R., 'Moynihan Offers Proposal to Preserve Social Security', *The New York Times*, 15 March 1998, p. 24. Moynihan would allow workers to pay only 12 per cent (instead of 14 per cent) of their income into the existing social security system; the other two per cent would be invested in a private investment vehicle.

19 'Catastrophic insurance' is an American term for protection against unusual medical expenses; e.g., from accidents or ravaging diseases. Expenses up to the limit of the 'deductible' are paid for out of the medical savings account. The higher the deductible, the lower the cost of the catastrophic insurance. To raise the 'deductible'—say, to $3,000, or even $5,000—would considerably lower the cost of the monthly cost for the insurance, and thus reserve more cash for the capital fund.

20 Presidential candidate Steve Forbes first brought the proportional income tax—or 'flat tax'—to prominence in the campaign of 1996, but Representative Dick Armey has introduced actual legislation for a flat tax plan of his own. Details in all such plans vary. The original proponents of the idea were Alvin Rabushka and Robert E. Hall in *The Flat Tax*, Stanford: Hoover Institution Press, 1985.

21 Hall, R.E., Rabushka, A., Armey, R., Eisner, R. and Stein, H., *Fairness and Efficiency in the Flat Tax*, Washington, DC: AEI Press, 1996. See also Hall and Rabushka, *The Flat Tax, op. cit.*

22 It seems patently more fair for everyone to pay at the same rate (the poor exempted) than at 'progressive' rates (higher rates as incomes rise). Those who think it more fair to have higher rates for higher incomes have never really justified that claim. They must face the fact that their odd sense of justice is frustrated by the sense of unfairness it raises in its targets and the wasteful search for tax shelters it encourages. For taxes to be paid fairly they must be perceived to have been levied fairly. I've been unable to locate good arguments for 'progressivity', although obviously the 'gut feeling' in their favour is widespread.

23 Ample materials are available from Citizens for Fair Tax, PO Box 27487, Houston, TX 77227-7497. Representative Archer has introduced his own version of the consumption tax in legislation before the Congress.

Anthony Giddens

1 Nickell, S., 'Unemployment and labour market rigidities: Europe versus North America', *Journal of Economic Perspectives*, Vol. II, 1997.

2 Ohmae, K., *The End of the Nation-State*, New York: Harper, 1994.

3 Hills, J., *The Future of Welfare*, York: Joseph Rowntree Foundation, 1997.

Paul Ormerod

1 Maddison, A., *Monitoring the World Economy, 1820-1992*, Paris: OECD, 1995.

2 For clarification, the growth rates represent average annual growth of the level of income from, for example, 1980 to the level in 1997. In other words, growth in 1980 itself is *not* included in the figure.

3 See, for example, the OECD, *Economic Outlook*, June 1993 for an assessment over a long period of the forecasting record of the G7 governments and the IMF.

4 Ormerod, P. and Rowthorn, R., 'Keep it in the family', *The Guardian*, 25 November 1996.

5 Though it is hard not to be amused by the account of Mr Novak's dinner party at which all the guests thought it reasonable that the Dow Jones would reach 11,000 by the year 2000. It recalls the claim of Shakespeare's Glendower that he can call spirits from the mighty deep. Anyone can, but how many come when you call, was the retort. And whilst Mr Novak's guests are entitled to their opinions, how many have backed their confidence by placing large amounts of their own money in the futures markets on their prediction?

6 Solow, R., Keynes Lecture, British Academy, 1997.

7 Japan's current problems stem from financial speculation in the late 1980s rather than labour market 'rigidities'.

8 For technical arguments as to why this is the case, see, for example, Ormerod, P., 'Problems of time-series econometrics', in Arestis, P., Grahl, J. and Daniel, S. (eds.), *Applied Economics: Festschrift for Bernard Corry and Maurice Peston*, Aldershot: Edward Elgar, forthcoming 1998.

Michael Novak: Rejoinder

1 Is the rock-bottom 'view' of social democracy as simple as this: 'Social democracy is the conviction that government is a crucial instrument for improving the lives of citizens in many areas; there must be a generous base of support below which government allows nobody to fall; as much as possible, life chances and enabling assets among citizens should be equalized (or, at least, flagrant inequalities

corrected); and perhaps other characteristics'? But do such principles amount to 'a view of the human being'? The phrase seems to strike deeper than this bare enumeration of convictions.

2   In *The Spirit of Democratic Capitalism*, IEA Health and Welfare Unit, 1991, I have tried to spell out the ideals and philosophical presuppositions of democratic capitalism. So, also, in 'The Constitution of Liberty', a philosophical outline in chapter ten of *Will It Liberate? Questions About Liberation Theology*, second revised edition, Lanham, MD: Madison Books, 1991. I would welcome a purely philosophical debate—vision against vision—attempting to clarify and compare these two rivals; or, perhaps, siblings of common parentage.

3   Berger, P., *The Capitalist Revolution*, New York: Basic Books, 1986, chapter 4.

4   Lloyd's crack about the dinner-table bet reflects the kind of cultural difference we need to bridge. When the bet was made, the Dow was at 6,500; not quite a year later it had climbed to 9,200 (2,700 points). With 30 months to go, another 1,800 points no longer seems improbable.

5   John Lloyd wickedly notes that the US has the lowest quotient of welfare and the highest quotient of violent crime. Nonetheless, as Giddens allows, welfare in Britain has different associations from those it has in American experience. Somewhere between 70 and 80 per cent of all violent crimes in the US are committed in high-welfare areas, especially among young males living in father-absent households. Superimposing a map of high crime areas over high-welfare areas on urban maps illustrates these correlations with stunning visibility. In recent years, after steps to reform the welfare culture and the culture of permissiveness, rates of violent crime have been falling precipitously: e.g., from more than 2,000 murders per year in New York City to under 800 per year. Europeans link crime in America to a relative lack of welfare; Americans link it with those areas where welfare programmes and rules are virtually all-embracing.

6   *Work Experience During Year by Selected Characteristics and Poverty Status in 1996 of Persons 16 Years Old and Over*, US Census Bureau.